D1035611

COVENANT OF TRUTH

BRITH EMETH

1959 5719

BRITH EMETH

IN MEMORY OF

PRESENTED BY

27575 SHAKER BOULEVARD, PEPPER PIKE, OHIO 44124

THE SPY FROM ISRAEL

THE SPY FROM ISRAEL

By BEN DAN

956.94
D19

VALLENTINE, MITCHELL — LONDON

ACKNOWLEDGEMENTS

Grateful acknowledgement is made for the use of the following
illustrations:

Plates 3, 7a and 7b by kind permission of Camera Press Ltd.
Plates 4 and 10 by kind permission of Associated Press Ltd.
Plates 5 and 6 by kind permission of Keystone.
Plates 8 and 9 by kind permission of United Press International
(U.K.) Ltd.

First published under the title
"L'Espion qui venait d'Israel"
by Fayard, Paris

First published in Great Britain 1969
by Vallentine, Mitchell & Co. Ltd,
18 Cursitor Street, London E.C.4.

© 1969 Ferenczy Verlag A. G. Zurich
SBN: 85303015 4

Printed and bound in Great Britain
by C. Tinling & Co. Ltd
Liverpool, London and Prescot

69-455

DEDICATED TO THE UNKNOWN
COMBATANTS FOR ISRAEL'S FREEDOM

CONTENTS

ILLUSTRATIONS

PUBLISHER'S FOREWORD

Elie Cohen, one of the most expert and resourceful secret agents in recent years, is a name known only to the most informed students of Middle East affairs. Yet it was due, in great measure, to this man that Israel, during the Six-Day War, defeated the forces of Syria within a matter of hours. And – unlike many master spies – he worked alone. There was no complex espionage network, no glamour, no James Bond heroics. But he had a cool efficiency and an uncanny ability to play a role basically alien to him, and to penetrate, by his unassuming brand of personal charm, the highest military and political circles in Syria. For three years he posed as an Arab from South America – until, one day, his secret transmitter radio was picked up by a detector car.

He was not allowed a defence lawyer during his trial, though two leading members of the French bar pleaded to be allowed to champion his cause. The Syrian authorities were merciless; the two lawyers were not even allowed to attend the trial, which was held in secret and without foreign press reporters. When Cohen was condemned to death, there were world-wide appeals for clemency, from such leading figures as the Pope, President de Gaulle, the former French Premier Edgar Faure, a group of British politicians, and others – but all in vain. Offers of ransom amounted to £85,000. The Israelis offered ten Arab agents, including several Syrians, in exchange for Elie's life. But they hanged him in public in Martyrs' Square in Damascus in May 1965.

It may be asked why the Syrian authorities were so intransigent. Wounded national pride was no doubt a factor; the real identity of the urbane, cultured "Kamal Amin Taabes" was never suspected by those who became his most intimate friends in Syrian government and defence circles. Some of them were, in fact, tried with him and had to pay dearly for their gullibility. But apart from that, the Arab fear of the Israeli Secret Service is deep and obsessive. It has become one of the most efficient in the world. It picks its men carefully, eliminating adventurers, boasters and would-be heroes. Discretion, observation, versatility and unobtrusive charm are vital ingredients – plus a dedicated sense of constructive patriotism. Elie Cohen possessed all these qualities, and more.

This is a true "spy story" which gives one a remarkable insight into the methods of the Israeli Intelligence system. It is also a human story of resourcefulness, courage and sacrifice. The late Israeli Prime Minister, Levi Eshkol, said: "Elie Cohen bore his fate with serenity and nobility; he died a hero's death". An inspiring truth in its own right; but more moving still when one considers the debt that his country owes to him.

1

THE FINAL NIGHT

Elie Cohen, the "Spy from Israel", was publicly executed in the main square of Damascus, the Martyrs' Square, at 3.30 a.m. on Tuesday, May 19, 1965. Damascus Radio, just before midnight, had first broadcast the news that he was to be hanged.

Just before midnight ... the warder's brisk step echoing down the passage, and the turning of the key in the lock of his solitary cell, had jerked him out of his sleep. He sat up with a start on his camp bed, still only half awake. In the weak glow of the night-light which was always kept burning, he could distinguish the outlines of two Syrian soldiers. Was he going to be tortured ...?

He was completely awake now. It was only then that he noticed Colonel Dalli, president of the special Military Court which had tried him, and Nissim Andabo, the 80-year-old Rabbi of Damascus, standing between the two soldiers. This unexpected visit brought him face to face with his impending fate; but he did not have time to react.

The colonel, a powerful-looking man, was ordering him to dress and stand to attention. His voice was guttural and pompous.

It was midnight on Monday, May 18, 1965, when Elie Cohen, standing to attention in the most closely-guarded cell in the el-Maza prison, heard Colonel Dalli say the fatal words:

"Tonight you will be hanged by the neck until you are dead."

The colonel, who had spoken in Arabic, stepped back to make way for the Rabbi. Bent with age and overcome with grief, the white-bearded old man recited, in a trembling voice, *El Maleh Rahemin*. The Hebrew prayer, the "Lord of Mercy . . ." the prayer which is recited for a man who is going to die.

Elie Cohen murmured the prayer with the Rabbi. The old man could not keep back his tears. When Rabbi Andabo lost all control and spoke the wrong part of the prayer, Elie gently corrected him.

In the military convoy which drove out of the prison gates into the warm, humid night nearly two hours later, across the sleeping city, the condemned man shared a covered van with the Rabbi and four Syrian soldiers armed with sten-guns. Elie could not see where the convoy was going, but he knew he would be hanged on that spot where, for centuries, the public gallows of Damascus had stood. A halt was made at the police station at the corner of Martyrs' Square. The people of Damascus had given it a rather ironic name: the Slaughter House. It was to be the condemned man's last stopping place.

Elie was taken briefly inside the police station and given a seat at a rough wooden table. He was told by Colonel Dalli that if he wished he might make his will or write a last letter. The prisoner turned to the Rabbi, who had been chanting psalms of praise to God, and said quietly: "I have no debts; I owe nothing to anyone; I do not want to make a will. But I have a last duty to my family; I should like to write them a letter."

He was given a pen and paper. Slowly and calmly, weighing every word, he wrote:

"My wife, Nadia, and dear family:
I am writing you these last words to entreat you to stay together.
I beg you, Nadia, to forgive me and to look after yourself and the
children. Make sure they get a good education. Take care of
yourself and them; see they want for nothing. Always stay on
good terms with my family.

Also, I would like you to marry again, so that the
children may have a father. You are entirely free to do this.
Don't, I beg you, spend your time crying over what is no more.
Always think of the future.

I send you all my last kisses; you, Sophie, Iris, Shaul,
and all my family. Don't forget a single one of them. Tell them
that my last loving thoughts were of them.

Do not forget, any of you, to pray for the salvation of
my father and the salvation of my soul.

My last kisses . . . Shalom.

Elie Cohen
18.5.65."

He had written these lines in Arabic. He thrust the sheet
of paper away from him, then thought better of it and took it
back. He used another sheet of paper to copy out the farewell
message – in French this time. As he had not been allowed to
write in Hebrew, he wanted to leave a French version so that
his last words to his wife and family should not survive in Arabic
only. Colonel Dalli put the two versions in his pocket and
indicated that it was time to go.

From the police station it was no distance to the floodlit,
heavily-guarded scaffold, wired off the centre of the square.
The Martyrs' Square has set the scene for every grim and
glorious event in the history of the Syrian Republic; countless
public executions, countless acclamations for the heroes of
successive coups d'état.

Three years earlier Elie Cohen had strolled here among

3

the Damascus crowds, inspecting the Israeli armoured half-tracks that Syrian troops had captured during the clash at Nukeib in the hills above the Sea of Galilee. Now it was to see him that the tense and silent onlookers, who had left their beds in all quarters of the city, were waiting – to gaze on the living Cohen, then the dead Cohen. He had been branded for three months past by the Syrian press as "a master spy", "a criminal without precedent", "a real fiend in human form". For millions of Syrian citizens the "Spy from Israel" had taken shape as an extaordinary being endowed with almost supernatural powers. Had he not managed for years to bamboozle the powerful military junta of Syria and outwit the complex organisation of its Secret Service?

He had, indeed, been an established figure in Damascus from January 1962 to January 1965. Only then did Syrian Intelligence officers burst into his flat and arrest him. From that moment he had been held completely incommunicado for a hundred days: no visitors, no Counsel, no letters. His trial, though parts of it had been televised, was held behind closed doors, apart from the opening sessions, and he had not been told whether anyone in the outside world even knew of his arrest.

He was naturally unaware of the Syrian Government's nervousness at the very time of his execution. The date had been fixed only 48 hours earlier, and advance knowledge had been given only to a minimum number of officers at the head of the military junta. The Syrian President, General Amin el-Hafez, had ordered Government, Party and Army leaders to be on call in Damascus. Secret reports had suggested that a death sentence passed on the spy would provoke an attack from Israel. The head of Syrian Military Security, Lieutenant-Colonel Ahmed Sweidani, had been recalled at 24 hour's notice from an official mission to Moscow. The Syrian frontier with Israel, from El-Hama in the south to the hills that face the village of Dan in the north, was reinforced that night with motorised units, batteries

Elie Cohen as Kamal Amin Taabes.

Elie Cohen (first on the left) as a child with his parents and brothers and sisters in Alexandria.

Elie and Nadia Cohen on holiday in Israel.

of guns and mortars. The soldiers manning Israeli posts on the frontier would follow, with their binoculars, the headlamps of strong military detachments moving into position on the hills in enemy territory.

The precautions were completely unknown to Elie Cohen as he stepped up from street level to the scaffold, brushing aside Colonel Dalli's offer of a supporting hand. Eyewitnesses close to the gallows – a group of some 50 journalists, cameramen and Syrian television technicians – observed that he was pale but calm when the giant hangman of Damascus, Abu Salim, without untying the prisoner's bound wrists, draped round him the coarsely-sewn white sackcloth used at executions.

All the members of the Military Court that had sentenced him were there to hear Colonel Dalli confront the spy with the question which had obsessed the Syrian leaders ever since his arrest: "Elie Cohen, did you have any accomplices in Syria? What have you to say?"

The group of bystanders then heard the condemned man repeat, once more, the only statement that had been wrung from him after weeks of torture: "I regret everything I have done, and I stand by my earlier statements." (An hour later Colonel Dalli was to explain this to the Press; Cohen meant to imply, according to him, that he had no Syrian accomplices.)

After making his statement, Cohen turned away from Colonel Dalli and went up the gallows steps. He declined the executioner's offer of a hood to pull over his eyes. The Rabbi recited for the last time the prayer, "Lord of Mercy". Four minutes later the hangman announced to the members of the Military Court that Elie Cohen was dead.

Colonel Dalli then attached to the white sackcloth shroud a large placard, the invariable last act of a Syrian execution. On it was written, in Arabic script, the sentence of the Military Court. It read:

"Eliahu Ben-Shaul Cohen was sentenced to death in the

name of the Arab people of Syria, having been found guilty of penetrating into a military sector and communicating secret information to the enemy".

Thus ended the extraordinary saga of Elie Cohen, who has become a legendary figure both in his own country and among its enemies. Ten thousand people filed past his body before the authorities removed it during the morning. It was buried in the Jewish cemetery of Damascus and lies there still. Requests that his remains should be handed over to his family in Israel have been repeatedly refused by the Government of Syria.

2

BOYHOOD AND YOUTH IN EGYPT

Elie Cohen was born in Egypt, where he lived till he was 32. During the last few years he spent there, he was separated from his family and wholly absorbed in a cause he had taken up as a young man – the emigration of Egyptian Jews to Israel.

The Cohen family originally came from Syria. They had lived for generations in Aleppo, in the northern part of that country; there had been a flourishing Jewish community in the town for hundreds of years. Early in the present century part of the Cohen family left Syria for Egypt – skirting Palestine, which was still under Turkish rule – and settled in Alexandria, where Elie was born in December 1924.

Like most oriental Jewish families, his parents gloried in the number of their offspring, most of them born in Alexandria. The eldest was a girl, Odette. Next came their firstborn son and pride of the family, Elie, named after the prophet Elijah – in Hebrew Eliahu. There were six younger children: Maurice, Ezra, Sarah, Sion, Ephraim and, lastly, Albert-Abraham.

The mother and father – he was a proud oriental Jew, fond of his traditional red fez – would spend whole evenings reminiscing about Aleppo in the Syrian dialect of their old home, but the six boys and two girls grew up as completely Egyptian

Jews. The Cohens could never have imagined that one day in 1962 the eldest son would find his way back to Aleppo as an Israeli spy, making a close study of the Syrian army officers' rising against the régime.

Elie Cohen, a slim, dark-haired boy, was sent to the Maimonides School run by the Alexandrian Jewish community. There he had his first Hebrew lessons, learning the language from the Sacred Books. He was an exceptional schoolboy, and passed on with a good basic education to Rabbi Ventura's Midrasha (Institute of Higher Hebraic Studies).

The good relations which existed at the time between Alexandria's Jewish community and their Arab neighbours had a rather different effect on the Jewish minority from the reaction produced in a similar situation in the West. Far from assimilating into the overwhelming Moslem majority, the Jews of Alexandria exerted themselves to preserve their own traditions and pass them on to future generations. Thus all the Cohen children, headed by Elie, attended a Jewish communal school from infancy onwards. The heritage of Judaism, the study of the Bible and the Holy Books, the reading of commentaries on the written and oral traditions, the maintenance of everyday rites and customs and the observance of the strict laws that regulate the life of orthodox Jews with an almost clockwork precision – all this, in Alexandria, was passed on from father to son.

However, Elie Cohen, who in no time was promoted to the status of "Iluj" (senior pupil), was not content to be just a Judaic scholar. He devoted much of his time to studying the language and literature of the Arabs, and also learned to speak excellent French, expressing himself in that language no less fluently than in Hebrew and Arabic.

His school friends describe him as different from the other boys. He seldom took part in the impromptu games of football in the break, but generally retired into a corner and looked through a lesson or re-read a page of one of the books he always carried around. His only sporting activities at the time were swimming off the coast and running along the sands.

He had just turned 18 when the Second World War reached Egypt's frontiers. Rommel's armies were at the gates of Alexandria in 1942, and Italian bombers would often fly over the city, attacking the port, one of the main Allied naval bases in the Mediterranean.

Alexandria's Jewish community saw the situation in a very different light from the Arab population, most of whom were ready to welcome Rommel's troops with open arms. The proximity of the Germans filled the Jews with foreboding.

One of Cohen's classmates, David Croudo, now an economic adviser in Tel Aviv, recalls that young Elie paid little attention to the frequent air-raid warnings. He treated them as a joke, and sometimes did not even bother to join his friends in the school air-raid shelter. He was already remarkable for his imperturbability at eighteen, and was never afraid of running risks. David Croudo remembers how, in moments of stress, Elie would turn to his unnerved classmates and reduce the tension with a joke.

But there was something about this studious, rather reserved boy that kept him apart from his fellows. He was ready, without a second thought, to give a helping hand to anyone who found it hard to understand the lessons, and (with a disregard of school rules that is still remembered) he would pass round during examinations the answers to questions liable to stump less gifted classmates. On the other hand, they are unanimous that he kept himself to himself and took little part in the life around him. Today, more than twenty years later, his schoolfellows still describe him as "an odd chap".

A rather simpler explanation of his reserve is possible. He was industrious and somewhat remote because his economic background differed from theirs. His father's small tie-shop in Alexandria did not make enough to keep a family of eight children, so Elie, as the eldest son, had to help. He earned his own school fees by working out of school hours for a cousin who had a clothing business. He could not afford to go to films, and he never acquired the habit, as his friends did, of buying a hot stew for lunch from the Jewish stall-keeper's portable oven in the school yard.

However, he took up a hobby at this period which became his craze and was to prove invaluable when he was sent to Syria. For his barmitzvah* in 1937 the 13-year-old boy was given a small Kodak box camera. This enthralled him so much that he carried it about everywhere and was always taking snapshots, especially after the birth of his youngest brother, Albert-Abraham. An album filled with the photographs he took of the baby and the rest of the Cohens is now one of the family's most treasured relics.

Another pastime that helped develop his powers of observation was the schoolboy game of spotting the makes and vintages of cars. He would spend hours on the balcony of the family flat watching cars go by and learning to recognise American and European models, coveted even then by young people. He very soon learned to distinguish R.A.F. Spitfires from German Messerschmitts during dogfights over Alexandria. He pinned photographs of fighter aircraft above his bed; 20 years later he was to provide Israeli Army Intelligence with the first pictures of Soviet Migs acquired by the Syrian Air Force.

His perceptiveness was developed, too, by another favourite game he played with his schoolfellows. This consisted in looking at an object for a limited time and then covering it up and drawing it from memory in the greatest possible detail. This practice was a kind of recreational extension of the teaching system in Jewish schools, where pupils had to learn whole chapters of the Bible by heart and long strings of formal prayers.

* Confirmation.

His years at Rabbi Ventura's school made him an obvious candidate for the Rabbinate. Every time the Rabbi was away for one reason or another, Elie took his place. "He has the makings of a genius", the Rabbi once told his parents, urging that he should be entered for the Rabbinical Seminary in the island of Rhodes.

Later, rather ironically, the Israeli Secret Service coined the humorous maxim: "Never expect a Rabbi to turn into a spy; but a spy, if pushed to it, may well pose as a Rabbi."

Elie did not become a Rabbi. Without dropping his Jewish studies, he developed a taste for mathematics and physics, and wanted to become an engineer. After leaving Rabbi Ventura's school he passed the entrance examinations for Farouk I University in Alexandria, specialising in applied electricity.

During these last eventful years of the war, world affairs, as well as developments in Egypt, forced themselves on his attention. Reading the local press and listening to the general gossip about the Egyptian régime, he often made bitter comments to his schoolfellows on the young King Farouk and his notorious life of luxury and pleasure.

Given his home environment and education, Elie was bound to take a particular interest in the life of the Jews in Egypt and in the Jewish National Home in Palestine, at that time under the British mandate. Like other young Alexandrian Jews, he was very soon familiar with the existence of Jewish Resistance or terrorist groups – the Haganah, the Irgun and the Stern Gang. Whispered reports of anti-British activities by one or other of these circulated among the Jews of Alexandra, and detailed descriptions of their exploits often appeared in the Egyptian press. Moreover, Egypt was one of many countries where these organisations maintained contacts, and the large Jewish community in Alexandria offered shelter to a number of agents from Palestine.

The first serious impact on Elie of the Jewish struggle in Palestine occurred in 1944. Two young Palestinian members of the Stern Group – Eliahu ben Zuri and Eliahu Hakim – had assassinated Lord Moyne in Cairo in order to focus world attention on the refusal of His Majesty's Government to allow large-scale Jewish immigration into Palestine. Elie Cohen followed the trial of the two young terrorists, and admired their fortitude in refusing to disclose the names of their comrades.

The two Eliahus, who are now legendary figures in Israel's history, were of his own age when they were hanged, and had the same first name as himself. It is not surprising that he came to identify himself with their struggle and death-sentence.

3

SABOTAGE IN CAIRO

From the time of his enrollment in the Zionist Youth of Alexandria in 1944, when he was 20, to the day of his execution in Damascus, Elie Cohen worked tirelessly for the Zionist movement and later for Israel. It was his vocation. He was steeped in Jewish and Hebrew culture, profoundly stirred by the death sentences passed in Cairo on the two Stern Group youths, resolved to serve the cause of his people. The idea of service had both a concrete and a symbolic meaning for him from the start.

Two Zionist Youth movements were active and spreading in Alexandria in 1944. There was the Maccabi, basically a sports organisation rather than an ideological body. On the other hand, the Hechalutz covered a variety of Zionists movements with differing ideologies and political trends. Such movements, some of them decidely leftish, would have found it difficult to reveal their activities openly in Egypt.

Their nucleus was Habonim, a branch formed for Jews outside Palestine of Hakibbutz Hameuhad, a socialist organisation inside Palestine that disseminates abroad the kibbutz ideal and the policy of the Mapai socialist party. Habonim's leaders were also in constant touch with Haganah, the semi-official Jewish defence organisation in Palestine.

13

Elie Cohen was able to give them valuable assistance. His age, contacts and upbringing rapidly fitted him to instruct, and then to lead, a group of boys and girls affiliated to this movement. He distinguished himself in particular by "missionary" work among young Alexandrian Jews who had not yet been won over to Zionist views, urging them to join the movement and get ready to leave for Palestine.

He himself was most strongly influenced at this time by Sammy (Samuel) Azzar, a young schoolmaster who had brought him into the Zionist movement. All Haganah activities in Egypt revolved round Azzar, and all the threads of Egyptian-Jewish emigration to Palestine and, after 1948, to Israel, passed through his hands.

This guide, philosopher and friend within the movement encouraged Elie Cohen to take an active part in the Zionist venture. Elie's zeal eventually aroused the suspicions of the Egyptian authorities; they discovered that he had joined the Zionists who had been engaged since 1945 in organising Jewish migration to Palestine. He was compelled to leave the Farouk I University in 1947, before finishing his course. From then on he devoted most of his time to intensive underground Zionist activities, earning his living as an accountant in a timber firm in Alexandria.

Israel's Declaration of Independence and the ensuing war waged against the Jewish State in 1948 by the Arab countries had severe repercussions on Egypt's Jewish population. Most of the 300,000 Jews still in the country soon realised that their only safe course, in the circumstances, was to get away. Ways and means for this mass-migration had been established well in advance, and involved the very organisations in which Samuel Azzar and Elie Cohen were at work.

Several emigration centres had been set up in Egypt. They were directed and financed by the Jewish Agency for Palestine, which was the Zionist movement's executive and formed a kind of shadow Government for the Jewish State. The head office was disguised under the name of the Grunberg Travel Agency, which occupied one floor of the imposing Immobilia building in Cairo and there was a branch office in Alexandria.

The clandestine emigration was really run on simple lines: "tourist" trips were organised to France, and those Egyptian officials who were too sophisticated to swallow the story about Jewish tourism to Europe had their palms suitably greased. The French consulate in Alexandria was induced to issue quite a number of French passports to those who still found it difficult to obtain Egyptian exit visas. Once they got to Europe, by whatever route, Egyptian Jews were shipped to Israel from Marseilles, Genoa or Naples.

All Elie's family left for Israel in this way. Odette, Maurice and Ezra went in 1949, followed by the others in 1950, He himself promised to join them as soon as his duties were fulfilled. In fact, he had to stay in Egypt for another six years, narrowly dodging at one point the gallows of Cairo, that claimed his closest friend.

This grim episode, in which he was fairly directly involved, had its beginnings in 1951, while Farouk was still on the throne. An atmosphere of war still pervaded the Middle East and, to forestall a threatened attack from Egypt, Israel set about assembling a first-rate Intelligence system there. A specially trained agent was sent in by way of Paris for the purpose of contacting and recruiting a ring of Egyptian-Jewish well-wishers who "could be relied on in an emergency". This agent, an officer of the Israeli Army (Tsahal) called Avraham Dar, passed under the name of "John Darling" for the purpose of his duties in Egypt.

"Darling" got into the country without difficulty in 1951 on a forged passport, and over the next two years he succeeded in recruiting a fair number of young Egyptian Jews who had volunteered to help Israel. He engaged some of them on espionage work, but they were rather amateur recruits, since they had not been trained in the special centres functioning in Israel since 1948. The rest of them remained in the underground Zionist movement, principally working for the Grunberg Travel Agency. One of Darling's jobs – though not his main duty – was to speed up Jewish emigration from Egypt.

One can observe now, after 15 years, that the group of unpaid volunteers who worked under Dar (or "Darling") was just made up of idealistic Jews who constituted no danger to Egypt and were of little help to Israel. However, part of the group was to be drawn into more dangerous, though hardly more useful, acitivities, as a result of major political developments in Egypt.

King Farouk had been overthrown and replaced by a revolutionary Government headed by General Neguib. Neguib was deposed, in his turn, by a military junta led by Colonel Nasser, who had seen active service against Israel. Nasser (who is still responsible for his country's destinies today), had opened negotiations with London in 1953 for an agreement which was to end in the complete withdrawal of British troops from the Canal Zone, leaving all British civilian and military supplies, installations and army camps in Egyptian hands.

The changed situation in Egypt naturally aroused some justified anxiety in Israel, where the danger from Colonel Nasser was recognised. He had been defeated and taken prisoner by Israeli troops in the Negev in 1948, and his desire for revenge was no secret.

The first Israeli Prime Minister and Minister of Defence, David Ben-Gurion, had temporarily retired from the Government, and was living at Sdeh Boker, a kibbutz in the Negev. The new Prime Minister and Foreign Minister, Moshe Sharett, announced at the end of 1953 that Israel was directly affected by the withdrawal of British troops from Suez. The British

Government tried to reassure the Israelis, but made no positive commitment likely to dispel their fears.

At this point the new Israeli Defence Minister, 50-year-old Pinhas Lavon, came into the picture. What has ever since, rightly or wrongly, been known as the "Lavon Affair" hinged on the action then taken in Egypt. Ten years later this notorious dispute was to bring about Ben-Gurion's final departure from the Government and a split in his party, the Mapai.

The point at issue was a series of acts of sabotage carried out in Egypt under the direction of "Darling", in which Samuel Azzar and other Egyptian-Jewish volunteers, among them Elie Cohen, were involved. The Government of Israel has never officially acknowledged the existence of this plot, or of the events to be described in this chapter, so we shall quote from the "American Universities Field Staff Report" for May 1961 the account of the episode given, after research, by Mr. E. A. Bayne.

"As Minister of Defence under the unwritten Israeli constitution (he writes), Lavon was charged with the protection of the nation. Defence can be conducted in several ways at once, obviously: by keeping powder dry; by preventive action, either limited or extensive (and Israel has undertaken both); and even by coercing allies. An idea along the last line seems to have occurred to the Israeli Military Intelligence, whose chief was Colonel Benyamin Gibli who was later appointed Military Attaché in London. This somewhat Machiavellian scheme is at the heart of the Lavon Affair."

Mr. Bayne, having discussed the British policy of withdrawing from Egypt to Cyprus, remarks that the idea hatched in the Israeli Defence Ministry in response to this eventuality "was terroristic, but it had its own amoral logic". The plan devised at Tel Aviv, he explains, was intended to exploit British public uneasiness arising from the withdrawal from Suez, and to shake American confidence in Nasser's supposed pro-Western trend.

17

"A black theory emerged: why not cause the destruction of certain American and British assets in Egypt, and particularly in Cairo, endangering British and American lives? The public outcry in Britain and the U.S. would be sufficient, hopefully, to cause a change of policy, so long as the plot could be made to seem to have been Egyptian-inspired. It would prove the irresponsibility of Egypt ... and the West would be forced to retain its own protection of the vital Canal."

These ideas were weighed up and studied at the Israeli Defence Ministry without the knowledge of the Prime Minister or even the Commander-in-Chief of the Army, General Moshe Dayan, worse, the plan was actually set in motion, and neither the Government nor its Prime Minister knew anything of it.

A second Israeli agent was sent to Egypt early in 1954, to join "John Darling", who had been forming activist groups there (with Azzar and Cohen among them) since 1951. The new agent had entered the country on a German passport under the name of Paul Frank, purporting to represent an important German firm dealing in electronic appliances. He had the double assignment of worming his way into Egyptian Government circles, so as to glean the maximum amount of information needed by the Israeli Secret Service, and of co-operating with Darling in the preparation of sabotage operations to be triggered off on orders from Tel Aviv.

Paul Frank succeeded in his first assignment beyond all expectations. He made friends in 1954 with some genuine German experts working for Nasser's army, and managed to get to know several high officials, especially those concerned with Egyptian Security. He was to be seen at that time in the company of Zakaria Mohieddin, later Prime Minister of Egypt, and of Admiral Soleiman. He even cultivated Colonel Osman Nury, then Head of Military Intelligence.

On the other hand, Darling, Paul Frank and the young

Egyptian Jews involved in their plot failed to carry out Tel Aviv's "Machiavellian design". After two months of preparation the two Israeli spies triggered off a succession of minor and quite amateurish acts of violence and sabotage in July 1954. A crudely-constructed explosive device set fire to the letter-box of an American subject. Another equally harmless bomb was let off on a shelf in the Cairo library of the United States Information Service. Finally, a matchbox filled with explosive went off in the coat-pocket of a 19-year-old youth called Natanson, just as he was going into a Cairo cinema where he was to plant it.

The consequences of these "sabotage operations", hastily improvised in the Cairo area by the two Israeli instructors and the young Eyptian Jews were out of all proportion to the material damage caused or the negligible political results achieved by these fatuous manoeuvres. The Egyptian secret police was able to lay hands at once on almost the entire ring of "spies and saboteurs working for Israel". Among the eleven rounded up were young Dr. Marzouk of the Jewish Hospital; Samuel Azzar, Elie Cohen's schoolmaster friend; Marcelle Ninio, a girl in the Grunberg Travel office; and Max Bennet, a German Jew, unconnected with the sabotage campaign, who had been sent to Egypt by Israeli Intelligence and had rendered them invaluable service.

Bennet had come into Egypt as the representative of a German firm specialising in artifical limbs for wounded soldiers, and had managed to establish contact with General Neguib himself. Tel Aviv was for a long time unaware that he had fallen into Egyptian hands as a result of another blunder of the Darling-Frank group: they had lost contact with him for a period, and despite strict orders that he was to carry out his Intelligence duties quite independently of other groups under their command, they instructed Marcelle Ninio, the Grunberg Travel girl, to trace him. It appears that she had been indiscreet enough to have more than one meeting with the lone spy.

Once the sabotage ring had been discovered by the Egyptian secret police, it did not take them long to arrest Max Bennet. "John Darling" was already in Europe, and Paul Frank left Egypt for Germany a few days later.

Elie Cohen, who had been arrested in 1952 for "Zionist extremist activity", but released after intensive questioning, was one of the sabotage team; indeed, he had rented an apartment in Cairo in his own name in 1953, at Samuel Azzar's request, for the group's under-cover work. When the whole ring, including his friend Azzar, was arrested in 1954, he was again questioned, but managed to persuade the police that he was innocent.

The arrest of the "saboteurs" was hardly mentioned in the Egyptian or Israeli newspapers, but for political reasons Nasser's Government gave far more publicity to their trial, which opened on December 7, 1954, than to their alleged outrages at the time. Just before the case ended Max Bennet committed suicide in his Cairo prison cell. On January 27, 1955, the court passed sentence. Marzouk and Azzar were condemned to death and executed four days later; two of their accomplices, Levi and young Natanson, received life sentences; Marcelle Ninio, who had protested in court, in the presence of the press, that she had been tortured in prison, was given 15 years' hard labour, and so was another of the accused, called Dassa. Two further defendants received seven-year sentences, and two were acquitted.

Elie Cohen had to stay on in Egypt till 1956. When Israeli troops invaded the Sinai desert late in October of that year, and British aircraft bombed Egypt to cover the landing of the British and French troops, he knew it was time to clear out at all costs. Like most Jews still in Egypt, he had been arrested as soon as the Suez operation started, and interned in a Jewish school building in Alexandria. After the failure of the Allied operation he was released, and at the end of the year he managed

General Amin el-Hafez, who refused to reprieve Elie Cohen, in the heyday of his power.

Rumana Street, Damascus, in the district where Elie Cohen had his flat.

to get away by the underground route he had used for so many others. After a brief intermission in Europe, he arrived in Israel at the beginning of 1957.

Something more should be said about another character in this drama, Paul Frank, who is now in prison – not in Egypt, as might be supposed, but in Israel.

Frank, evading the Egyptian police in July 1954, had, as we have seen, returned to Germany. Thanks largely to a faked record as an S.S. man, he continued to do valuable work there and in Austria for the Israeli Secret Service, in which he was up-graded. However, the time came when he was ordered to break off all contact with Egyptians in Europe. Despite his instructions, it was discovered that he still had meetings with Egyptians, including his old acquaintance Admiral Soleiman, who had been transferred to a diplomatic post in Bonn. By now there was some suspicion that Frank was working for the Egyptians too.

He was brought back to Israel, tried by a military court in Jerusalem, and sentenced in 1959 to 12 years' imprisonment. During the inquiry the 1954 affair in Cairo came up again, and at this point the Israeli Secret Service reached the horrifying conclusion that as far back as 1954 Frank had been working with Egyptians and acting as a double agent. In that year he seems to have told them the object of his assignment, including the political sabotage, and to have been paid 40,000 DM (£3,400) for his information. His treachery would explain how he managed to leave Egypt after the 1954 arrests.

Nor was this all. In the course of his interrogation in Jerusalem, Paul Frank accused two Israeli officers of having made him falsify his evidence about the incidents in Cairo during 1954, their purpose being to use this twisted evidence to throw responsibility for the abortive plot on the Defence Minister at the time, Pinhas Lavon. Mr. Lavon had been forced out of office in 1955, in favour of Mr. Ben-Gurion.

Paul Frank's new evidence blew up a major storm over Israel in 1960–1, which burst out again in 1964. As a public scandal the "Lavon-Ben-Gurion Affair" left a trail of bitterness behind it. It raged across the country, uprooting Lavon (now permanently retired from public life), splitting the Mapai party, and causing the withdrawal from the Government of Ben-Gurion, Dayan and Shimon Peres (Under-Secretary for Defence) who together formed a splinter group known as Rafi.

The upheaval was lengthy and painful. But after all the official and unofficial commissions of inquiry, the responsibility for the 1954 disaster, which caused the deaths of Max Bennet the spy and the militants Marzouk and Azzar, and the long prison sentences* inflicted on Marcelle Ninio and other Egyptian Zionists, is still a matter for dispute.

---

* They were eventually released early in 1968, as part of an exchange of prisoners arranged by the United Nations mediator, Gunnar Jarring.

4

ADJUSTING TO ISRAEL

The Cohen family had settled in Bat Yam, south of Tel Aviv. It was a modern suburb, by the sea, with blocks of flats rising from the sandy soil near the rocky coast. Being so near Tel Aviv, with its possibilities for jobs or trade, Bat Yam attracted thousands of newcomers from Europe, North Africa and Egypt, and the district was a babel of multifarious languages and traditions.

Almost nothing had been heard from Elie for six years. Occasionally a new arrival brought some scraps of news about his secret Zionist work, and once the Cohens had a postcard from Italy, from a friend of his, telling them he was well and still in Alexandria. One day then, early in 1957, he landed at Haifa with the last batch of Jews from Egypt. All the possessions he had managed to bring out filled a single suitcase.

His first call was on his brother Maurice at Ramat Gan adjoining Tel Aviv. Maurice was out, so Elie went on to his parents' flat at Bat Yam, where he heard his youngest brother, Albert-Abraham, ask his mother who this gentleman was. The child could not recognise his big brother after six years, but his question had a deeper significance. Elie remained a stranger to his family for a long time, and found it very difficult to adapt himself to their new environment.

The years of separation and underground work in Egypt formed a barrier. So did his school Hebrew, too literary for everday purposes in Tel Aviv. But there was another factor, perhaps the most important: his reserve, noticeable even in childhood, had grown deeper.

It is worth observing that he systematically refused to discuss with his relatives the details of what they called his Egyptian "adventure" – his periods under arrest, the celebrated sabotage affair, the vicissitudes of illegal emigration. Some years later one of his brothers remarked that Elie used to keep his secrets locked up, as it were, "in a safe inside him that nothing could open".

Newcomers with an excellent theoretical knowledge of the Jewish State often find it hard to adjust themselves to everyday life without a lengthy struggle. So it was with Elie, who was by no means at home in Israel at first. During the first few months he sought out old friends from Alexandria who were scattered about the country, and tried to pick up the threads.

In the room his parents had kept for him in the family flat he arranged a miniature dark-room where he could develop his films; he was still as enthusiastic about photography, as he had been in Egypt ten years earlier. Among the subjects he photographed was the military parade on Israel's Independence Day in 1957, when the Army put on show for the first time the mass of Egyptian and Soviet equipment captured during the Sinai campaign.

He used these months, while he was adapting himself, to improve his Hebrew, English and French, and to gain practice in four other languages of which he had learnt the rudiments at night classes in Alexandria – Spanish, German, Greek and Italian. As before, his favourite reading consisted of text-books on electronics, supplemented now by French novels. One can assume that he found it hard at this time to forget his years in Egypt and the friends who had been hanged: the street at Bat Yam where he lived with his parents is called "The Street of the Cairo Martyrs".

He did not find a job till the end of 1957, and it was certainly no mere chance that his first employment was in the Ministry of Defence, where there were senior officers familiar with his under-cover work in Egypt. With his knowledge of languages, he was taken on as a translator, but after a relatively short trial, he was dismissed. Excellent as his classical Hebrew – the language of the Bible and of prayer – had always been, his knowledge of modern colloquial Hebrew was considered inadequate for translating press-cuttings.

Early in 1958 he found a new job, which presented no such problem. He was engaged as an accountant by Hamashbir, the central marketing agency of Histadruth, the Israeli trade union organisation. Here his work was greatly valued, and he was given repeated commendation and rapid promotion.

He was now self-supporting and felt more at home. During 1958 he made a number of excursions within the country, visiting, for instance, the Negev, Sodom and the port of Eilat. In 1959 he took his first look at the Syrian frontier, which was becoming the sensitive defence sector now that the Sinai campaign had brought incidents on the Egyptian border to a halt. Skirmishes, clashes between patrols, infiltrations by Syrian terrorists and, later, real frontier expeditions by both sides, had started in 1958–9.

Elie knew some of the members of the Army Club, established at Tel Aviv for men on leave and their friends. Here he met his future wife, Nadia, an attractive new arrival in Israel from Iraq, who had a pioneering zest akin to his own. They made up their minds quickly, and were married in August 1959. The religious ceremony at Bat Yam was followed by a large family celebration. They settled in a small flat in Bat Yam, and Elie continued with his accountancy job at Hamashbir.

Then, one evening, Nadia recalls, Elie came home and said briefly:

"I'm leaving Hamashbir I've been offered a better job – an agency with a large commercial concern. It will mean travelling abroad from time to time."

He did not tell her what kind of concern it was; he would have found it hard to explain why he called it commercial. Nor did he explain why he had chosen, a few days after announcing his change of occupation, to start growing a moustache. The "concern" was the Israeli Secret Service.

5

THE ISRAELI SECRET SERVICE

Despite all the "revelations" that appear in the news-papers from time to time, the Israeli Secret Service keeps the world, including its fellow-citizens, very much in the dark. Ultimate control rests with the Prime Minister, who has also been Minister of Defence for most of the past twenty years. Agents employed by the Israeli Secret Service are, except for those seconded from the Army, civil servants who are paid the normal salary of their civil service grade, on a scale agreed between the Government and the Union of Public Employees. Departmental heads draw up to 1,600 Israeli pounds (£190 sterling) a month; junior officials or agents start at about one-third of this salary. So there is no scope for living on the James Bond scale; an Israeli secret agent's life, on duty or off, at home or abroad, does not run to luxury hotels, baccarat tables or racing cars.

The origins of the Israeli Secret Service date back to the heroic period of Jewish Settlement in Palestine. At the beginning of the present century the settlers, faced by Arab attacks, were compelled to form a common defence organisation, which subsequently acquired the title of Hashomer (the Watchman). As the Jewish population of Palestine grew and the dream of a

27

"National Home" came nearer to reality – though well before the events which were to speed up the creation of an independent Jewish State – a real underground army, known as Haganah (Defence) established a network embracing every town, village and settlement in the country.

It was obviously necessary to build up, in conjunction with Hashomer and Haganah, an embryonic Intelligence Service which could give warning of attacks by bands of Palestinian Arabs, and keep an eye on the activities of terrorist leaders who had established themselves in neighbouring countries. This embryonic Secret Service was known even before the end of the British Mandate as Sherut Yediot or "Shay", meaning just Intelligence Service.

When an independent Israel was created in 1948, not only were Haganah and Shay incorporated in the Defence system of the new State, but also the so-called terrorist self-defence movements such as the Irgun (Etzel) and the Stern Group, with their respective Intelligence services. Along with the formation of a professional, highly efficient Israeli Army came reorganisation of Secret Service functions to meet the requirements of a nation surrounded on all sides by hostile states sworn to its destruction.

From the start, intense care and strict secrecy were essential for this indispensable arm of the new State, which occupied a narrow strip of land with disproportionately long frontiers. The Intelligence Service provided a king of defence in depth, extending into the heart of neighbouring countries.

In this part of the Middle East the whole future of a nation could be determined in a few hours. The business of the Intelligence Service is consequently to anticipate the changes, moves and course of action likely to be adopted by those in civil or military authority on the other side of the frontier. Thus the Israeli Secret Service operates for the most part abroad in neutral or enemy territory, rather than at home.

Apart from some minor departmental changes made in 1964, the Service retains the permanent structure that it acquired in 1950, with five main branches:

(1) The Intelligence and Research Service, known as Mossad, whose agents work mostly abroad.

(2) The Army Intelligence Service, called Modi'in – the military branch of the Secret Service, concerned only with the operations of the armed forces of countries hostile to Israel.

(3) Israel's Internal Security Service, known as Shin Beth – the Hebrew initials of Sherutei Habitahon (meaning Security Services). This name is often wrongly used for Israel's Secret Service as a whole, whereas it really denotes only the Counter-Espionage Service inside Israel.

(4) A Research and Information Department that forms an integral part of the Foreign Ministry in Jerusalem, but co-operates with the rest of the Secret Service and pays particular attention to political information regarding the Arab countries.

(5) An Investigation Branch of the Israeli Police Force, with special responsibility for police duties connected with counter-espionage – taking the appropriate steps only when the Shin Beth has passed a case over for action by due process of law.

Because its agents operate abroad, Mossad is the most important branch of the Israeli Secret Service, and it is Mossad or one of its agents that is involved whenever the world press attributes some incident to Israel's espionage service. Indeed, such operations as the capture of Adolf Eichmann or the tracking down of German scientists working for Egypt were carried out by Mossad.

Each of the five branches is headed by a top civil servant or a senior officer in the Army or Police, as the case may be. The Secret Service system as a whole comes under a Supervisor of State Security Services (in Hebrew "Memuneh al Sherutei Habitahon") who co-ordinates the working of all five branches, and in addition personally directs Mossad. He presides at the weekly meeting of the heads of the Service, and takes the most important operation decisions; and he is responsible to the Prime Minister and Defence Minister for the Intelligence Service as a whole. His general policy has to be approved by a small committee of the Israeli Parliament – the Security Committee – and he is backed by a Ministerial Committee appointed by the Cabinet.

In Israel people attribute, almost as a matter of faith, an unerring, mystique of success to the nation's Secret Service and take it for granted that every one of its agents behaves heroically. It is fair to say that popular opinion all over the world pays Israeli Intelligence the same compliment. This judgment was particularly emphatic when news of the capture in Argentina of Adolf Eichmann broke upon an astonished world. It was a brilliant coup, though not really the most hazardous or most important achievement of the Israeli Intelligence Service: but it was virtually the first and perhaps the only major operation by agents from Tel Aviv to be given such resounding and detailed world publicity – even if the details were not always accurate.

Isser Harel, the former head of the Service, who is now an almost legendary figure both in Israel and abroad, has described the way in which its agents are selected.

"We would never take on (he says) any adventurer of the James Bond, film hero-type. We don't want adventurers or heroes in our Service, and we don't want any of the volunteers who so often approach us. As a rule it is we who suggest to a man that he might work with us. If he accepts the idea, we let him volunteer at that point to join the Service.

"Our reasoning in the matter is simple: the first point of interest to us in an agent is why he is out for 'adventure'. We want our men to be honest, devoted, loyal and patriotic – in

other words human – and, above all, modest. Annonymity for
the agent and total secrecy about his work are essental if we are
to succeed. Men who find it burdensome to remain anonymous
or are over-inclined to hint to outsiders that they are on secret
work are got rid of as quickly as possible."

The numerical strength of the Service – embracing both
administrative staff and agents in Israel and abroad – is
absurdly small, a few hundred at most. Their pay, as already
indicated is well below the level maintained in other countries
for similar work. But the men and women chosen – the overwhelming majority of them recruited from Israeli nationals, so
as to ensure the greatest patriotism and loyalty – are as a rule
highly qualified for their duties, both in character and in
ability.

A glance at the life of Isser Harel, who directed this
Service for more than ten years, may throw light on the qualities
that sustain it, while the attitudes of mind and sense of values of
its agents are tragically illustrated in the story of Elie Cohen,
who was recruited in Harel's time.

Harel, nicknamed "Isser Hakatan" (Little Isser) because
he was rather short, was originally called Halpern. He was born
in 1912 in the Russian town of Vitebsk, where Chagall came
from. The advent of the Bolsheviks forced his father, a small
manufacturer, to move to Latvia. In 1929 Isser Halpern, then
17, and belonging to a left-wing Zionist youth movement,
landed in Palestine with a single suitcase and a pistol he had
secretly acquired. He joined a kibbutz at Herzlia, near Tel
Aviv, and worked hard in the local orange groves for some
years. About 1942 he took the Hebrew name of Harel and
enlisted in the Palestine Supernumerary Police, a Jewish
Defence Force recognised and fostered by the British Mandatory
authorities.

His future was decided by a minor incident: a British
officer made insulting remarks about the Jewish religion, and

31

Harel (who had never had strong religious convictions) hit the officer full in the face, much as David smote Goliath. He was ordered to apologise, refused, and was discharged from the unit.

Shortly afterwards he became an agent for Shay, the Haganah's underground Intelligence Service. His new chief, David Shaltiel (who later served as Israel Ambassador in Holland), was quick to notice Harel's unusual capacity for analysing information, and made him responsible for the internal security of the underground organisation and, later, head of Shay for the Tel Aviv area. Here he met such Haganah leaders as Israel Galili, at present (1968) Minister without Portfolio, and Ben-Gurion.

From then on he rose rapidly in the Secret Service, passing from Shay to Shin Beth, the counter-espionage branch, which he directed from the foundation of the State of Israel till 1953, when Ben-Gurion, as Prime Minister and Minister of Defence, put the entire Secret Service in his charge with personal responsibility for Mossad.

He became the Prime Minister's most enigmatic, but most trusted adviser, a position he fully earned. His special gifts – his insistence that his men should combine a high moral character with exemplary professional keenness, and his own unbounded devotion to his duties – brought into being a Secret Service that made up in quality for its lack of numbers.

Few Israelis have a detailed knowledge of Isser Harel's career, and we shall certainly not know the full story before Israel and her Arab neighbours sign a lasting peace treaty. However, this much can be said at the present time: Harel made it a rule to expose himself to the dangers confronting his agents – a practice against which his colleagues frequently argued and which they criticised after his resignation in 1963. More than once he visited Arab countries personally.

His wife and children were never allowed to know exactly what his work was. His name was never uttered in

Israel nor his photograph published. Finally, it was he himself who planned Eichmann's kidnapping in detail; he took a personal part in his capture at Buenos Aires, escorted him in the Israeli aircraft that flew him away, and dashed from Lydda airport to Jerusalem to tell Ben-Gurion that Eichmann was now in Israel.

The Israeli Secret Service does not confine itself to spying in Arab countries, tracking spies in Israel or hunting former Nazis. There was the famous occasion in 1962 when Isser Harel was instructed by Ben-Gurion to recover a lost child. Little Joseph (Yossele) Schumacher had been kidnapped by his orthodox Jewish grandfather from his irreligious parents, and was not to be found in Israel.

Harel set up his headquarters in Paris, and methodically combed all Jewish institutions in France, Belgium, Switzerland and Holland. After six weeks, his agents found that Yossele had been hidden with a Rabbi in Brooklyn. Harel got in touch with the Israeli Ambassador in Washington, Avraham Harman, and asked him to get the United States Attorney-General, the late Robert Kennedy, to instruct the F.B.I. to take legal measures to free the child.

When the Ambassador hesitated for a moment on the telephone, for fear of legal complications, Harel, confident of the support of Ben-Gurion and Mrs. Golda Meir, the Foreign Minister, told him brusquely that he was not seeking his advice: "I am asking you to apply at once to Mr. Kennedy and do what you're asked to do." This move had the expected result, and the F.B.I. was instructed to set the child free and take care of him until he left for Israel.

Harel was a hard man, not given to compromise in his work. He resigned his position with Ben-Gurion in 1963 as the result of two incidents about which the general public is still ill-informed. The first, which no doubt led psychologically to the second, concerned Israel Ber, Ben-Gurion's military adviser, who was also the official military historian. Harel had insisted, in spite of Ben-Gurion's objections, on having this man closely watched by his agents.

It was soon proved that Harel had more judgment than his chief. To the consternation of Ben-Gurion and the public at large, Ber confessed that he had spied on Israel for years in the interests of a Communist power. Moreover, he had access to the country's most secret Defence files the whole time and, up to the day that Harel's men caught him, he enjoyed the complete confidence of his superiors.

Though this incident was entirely to Harel's credit, it nevertheless cast a shadow over his relations with Ben-Gurion, and the head of the Secret Service was drawn into the faction of Ministers and Mapai party leaders who had been anxious ever since the Lavon affair, to get rid of Ben-Gurion.

The final breach between the two men, who had admired and completely trusted each other for fifteen years, occurred over the affair of the German scientists. For years, Intelligence agents had kept the Government of Israel informed about the part played by former Nazis in Cairo in Nasser's political campaign against Israel. But after the defeat of the Egyptian Army in the Sinai desert in 1956 Nasser had called in a group of German scientists who had served the Third Reich.

The group included Professors Pilz and Goerke and other former members of the wartime V 1 (flying bomb) and V 2 (rocket) teams. They were being paid astronomical sums to produce for Nasser remote-controlled medium-range rockets that might prove fatal to Israel. However, their efforts caused no undue perturbation there. Possibly their capabilities were underestimated: their training was considered out of date, and they pretty certainly had not got all the scientific and technical data required to build modern rockets.

All the same, it became known in 1962 that Egypt possessed rockets to be reckoned with – admittedly not weapons accurate enough for remote control, but still rockets that could deliver explosive or even nuclear warheads on any target in Israel. This discovery touched off a lively international campaign that was once more directed personally by Isser Harel from a neutral base.

It is still too soon to confirm or refute Egyptian allegations that the Israeli Secret Service was responsible for all the machinations of that time: threatening letters to the scientists' families in West Germany, kidnappings, parcels posted in Hamburg to explode in Egypt, press campaigns in Europe and America, and intensified diplomatic pressure everywhere through Israeli embassies.

Harel, who had produced the information about the German scientists' work in Cairo, was given a free hand by Ben-Gurion. But the Prime Minister and his staff at the Defence Ministry came to realise in due course that Harel's campaign was going to compromise irretrievably the Ministry's unpublicised dealings with West Germany, which was at the time supplying Israel with considerable quantities of defensive arms of all types.

Ben-Gurion was compelled, as a matter of urgency, to haul Harel back at the height of his campaign, and explain the political and military damage it was causing. He demanded convincing proof that the German scientists had really furnished Nasser with "the decisive weapon" – as Harel, backed by Mrs. Golda Meir, the Foreign Minister, called it. Having been Ben-Gurion's confidential adviser for ten years, Harel was not used to having his information questioned or his word doubted.

Wild with fury, he turned on the Prime Minister: "You can get all the proof you need from my successor." With these words he slammed the door and left, and the next day it became public knowledge that he had resigned.*

* Harel came back in 1965 as Security adviser to Prime Minister Levi Eshkol, but resigned in the following year owing to a disagreement.

6

LEARNING TO BE A SPY

Not one of the hundreds of people walking up and down Allenby Street, the main thoroughfare of Tel Aviv, one summer day in 1960, paid much attention to a curious game that was being played by two men whose physical appearance contrasted strangely. One of them was Elie Cohen, tall and well-built. The other, a head shorter, but strong and sturdy-looking, with bushy eyebrows and a majestic moustache, was Cohen's instructor, who was to set him on the road from Tel Aviv to Damascus. Cohen addressed him by his first name, Yitzhak (Isaac), but sometimes used the nickname given him by his friends in the Secret Service – "The Dervish". (This is a Persian word which literally means a *beggar*, and is used throughout the Moslem world to describe mystics.)

Under the Dervish's directions, Elie was practising one of the many training exercises that he had to master before he could be finally despatched to an Arab country. The decision would not be one-sided: up to the last minute he was free to opt out. The Dervish had a habit of reminding him in a fatherly tone that if he had second thoughts, or doubts whether he could carry out his mission, he should say so, and they would call the whole thing off. The time spent in training would not be held against him. Yitzhak added in English: "No hard feelings".

The trainee spy, flushing, and keeping his temper, with difficulty, would reply quietly: "What do you think I volunteered for? Just to change my mind? How can you talk about second thoughts when the security of our country is at stake?" He had, like Yitzhak, a habit of ending the discussion with a catch-phrase which summed up his state of mind: "Why should I be considered more precious than all the men who are on enemy soil at this very moment?"

The two of them, Elie and the Dervish, had been walking up and down Allenby Street all the morning, with an occasional pause at a stall for a glass of fruit juice or a sandwich. It is a main thoroughfare; crowds gather round the shop-windows at midday and swarm around the entrances to cinemas. Elie knew that among the throng were two people whose job it was to follow him and that this exercise was a vital part of the training: Elie simply had to identify his two "shadows".

"Cross the road and walk along the pavement opposite," he was told. "Stop by a newspaper kiosk and look at the magazine photos; pause at a shop window; remember you're being followed everywhere and all the time. Try to spot them; but don't panic or lose your head; don't turn round; don't attract their attention or anyone else's." The Dervish made sure that Elie got the point: "To-day you're being followed by friends; to-morrow it'll be your enemies. You don't know who'll be shadowing you in Cairo or Damascus or Baghdad, when you'll have to face the enemy alone."

The Dervish was like that. His quiet instructions and explanations struck home like a knife-thrust. From the start of Elie's training, his tutor had systematically endeavoured to destroy his illusions. Without trying to frighten his pupil, he wanted him to realise the full dangers and brutal possibilities of his job, once it took him over Israel's frontiers.

By this method the Dervish intended to attain an objective of great importance to the success of Elie's mission. Every Secret Service knows how vital it is to a spy in enemy territory to have a close bond with his "control" at headquarters, to have confidence in him and to enjoy his confidence, so that the man in the field trusts the judgment of the man who gives him orders. The spy will then feel surer, more secure, and he will therefore act more boldly and effectively.

Indeed, the Dervish succeeded, in the course of a few months, in gaining Elie's confidence and establishing a current of mutual understanding and friendship between them. He had taken to Elie at their first meeting, but there was a long gap between the first spontaneous liking and complete mutual trust.

To explain how they came together, one must go back to the time when Elie was still working in the Ministry of Defence – going through the newspapers that arrived in Tel Aviv every day from Egypt, Syria and other Arab countries, and making translations into Hebrew. He often remarked to his colleagues that he would have preferred to be sent abroad, as he did not feel cut out for office work.

He had voiced this desire in the hearing of a certain Intelligence captain in charge of the translations section of the Ministry, who showed no reaction. However, some weeks later he observed casually: "I made inquiries in the right quarters, to see if they'd take you on. But I was told – and no offence meant! – that the principle of refusing volunteers applied to you as much as to others. They won't make an exception for you."

This first rebuff from the Secret Service was a great disappointment to Elie, and he confided his feelings to another translator called Zalman, who recalls his indignant question: "Why do I have to waste my time combing the Arab newspapers, when I could get hold of much more useful material on the spot?"

Cohen had no idea how closely Zalman had noted his words and how faithfully he passed them on. The Secret Service had already opened a file on him and was discreetly collecting information about Elie from various sources. Eventually his record was handed over to the Dervish, who decided early in 1960 to interview him.

One evening, when Elie got home from his work as an assistant accountant with Hamashbir, he was surprised to find Zalman waiting for him. The visitor apologised to Elie's wife, and walked down the street with him for what he described as a private business talk. At this point Elie was told for the first time that the Secret Service had, despite evidence to the contrary, taken note of his request and had now decided to consider his application.

"We've turned you down on two occasions. But now it's our turn to ask whether you're really prepared to join us. Are you willing, when the time comes, to go off on a mission to Europe, or even one of the Arab countries?"

That was the gist of Zalman's question, and he reported back to his superiors that Elie, "deeply stirred," had replied very briefly: "Just one reservation, I'm not keen on Europe. But I'll go to any *Arab* country you like."

Zalman observed to Elie that a future change in his private life – his wife was expecting a baby – might affect his decision. He pointed out, too, that his Secret Service salary would be ridiculously low: 350 Israeli pounds (£70) a month. In any case, no final decision had been taken, and he would have time and opportunity to back out.

Two days later Elie met the Dervish for the first time. This meeting, too, was in the evening after work. Zalman took him to a tumble-down house in Allenby Street near the main post office. They climbed up to an attic, where the paint was peeling all round the door. They rang the bell, and the Dervish appeared. "Call me Yitzhak," he said with a friendly grin.

Zalman left them, and the two men sat down in the typical bachelor's den and began to talk. There was an immediate sympathy between them.

"Why do you want to go abroad?" asked Yitzhak. "What's the urge for adventure? Aren't you happy at home? Are you trying to contract out of family life?"

Questions like that stung Cohen into protesting with emphasis that he was happily married and genuinely in love with his wife. He did admit that he had financial difficulties and found it hard to make ends meet on his salary from Hamashbir of 180 Israeli poinds (£36) a month, but the prospect of joining the Secret Service for mercenary reasons was repugnant to him. "I'm sure," he said, "that I can do our cause some good. Nadia will accept months of separation if I'm doing something worth while for the country, and if it's a job I really like."

The Dervish interrupted him: "Remember that if we take you on, neither your wife nor your family nor your friends will be allowed to know anything about what you're doing. If you succeed, you'll celebrate your triumphs by yourself or, occasionally, with your Mossad bosses. You are utterly forbidden to discuss any aspects of our Service with anyone. It's not just your life and death – it's the success of our work. As far as we're concerned, your life and our work are of equal importance."

Elie, feeling that he had blundered, tried to put things right: "There's no question of telling Nadia the truth about my job. I only meant that she would be happy about it if she felt that it was what I wanted, even if she didn't know what it was all about."

The Dervish told him his wife would have to believe, once and for all, that her husband was working for an import–export firm, in whose interests he would have to travel about both in Israel and abroad. "You'll have to lie to your wife. Are you sure you can? Won't these lies cause a rift between you?"

Yitzhak knew in his heart that no Secret Service in the world could stop its agents revealing the secret of their missions to their wives during the moments of intimacy that follow months of separation. Even so, he was in duty bound to give Elie the same sort of futile warning that other Secret Service instructors had to give their new recruits.

The two men went on talking in the Allenby Street attic far into the night. Yitzhak had Elie's file in front of him and questioned him systematically on all the points raised by those who had gone through his record before giving the green light for this first interview. He questioned him closely about the sabotage episode in Egypt and his subsequent arrest. It was clearly essential to establish what the Egyptians knew, or were in a position to find out, about Elie's life, and how easily they might trace him once he had crossed into an Arab country. Needless to say, the Israeli Secret Service had never contemplated sending him to Egypt, where he was known and labelled as a Zionist agitator.

The Dervish harped back to the motives that had induced Elie to apply for Secret Service work. Hadn't he been reading too many spy stories, and wasn't it this kind of reading that made him want to become a spy? Elie, determined once more to demonstrate his good faith, emphasised that he had just been rebuking his young brother Abraham for reading too many thrillers and neglecting his school books.

Yitzhak liked these straightforward replies. The Dervish was far from being a bureaucrat; before 1948 he had made his name in a clandestine "terrorist" movement. Now he had the instinctive feeling that Elie was just the man for the Secret Service.

Shortly before midnight he gave him several forms to fill up and sign, all headed "State of Israel: Ministry of Defence". They were questionnaires, to which his answers were already known. But the Dervish and his superiors needed Elie's formal signature, which he gave that night, thereby enrolling himself in the Israeli Secret Service.

Over the next few days, when he was given leave from Hamashbir, he was medically examined and graded A 1. He was also subjected to various psychological and personality tests, in which he got high marks.

Some weeks after the tests, Elie had a second meeting with the Dervish, who patted him on the back. "Things have gone very well for you so far, let's hope it lasts," he said. "We've still a long way to go. Now you must give up your job and place yourself entirely at our disposal. For six months you'll be put through a training course that will be extremely stiff and exhausting, physically and mentally. If we still want to work together after that – you, as well as we – we'll make further plans. As from to-day you'll be getting 350 Israeli pounds (£70) a month." That day Elie came home in good spirits. He told Nadia he'd just been taken on by a commercial firm for which he would, when required, be going abroad. Nadia did not ask any awkward questions.

He then set about doing something the Dervish had asked of him – growing "a fine moustache, at least as good as mine." (The Dervish had owned for 30 years a splendid, awe-inspiring moustache, now somewhat unkempt and yellowed round the edges from chain-smoking.) Elie had never been tempted to display what is considered in the East a proof of virility. However, he assured his startled family that he had sworn not to shave his upper lip till Nadia produced a son.

They had just had their first child, a baby girl whom they named Sophie. But his wife knew how much he wanted a son.

We return to Elie walking up and down Allenby Street with the Dervish, trying to identify and unmask his "shadows". At first he failed repeatedly. The exercise was continued for days on end without his once discovering the "agents" following him. Yet every time, after the exercise, the Dervish would produce snapshots they had taken of Elie in front of a newspaper kiosk or shop window. He was even shown film sequences of himself strolling along, still unable to distinguish out the "shadows" from other passers-by.

After a week's practice Elie managed for the first time to pick out the men trailing him. From then on the exercise was a game, and it became increasingly easy for him to spot them. He was learning, thanks to the Dervish's hints, to throw them off, while they adopted all kinds of manoeuvres to take him unawares with their miniature cameras.

Towards the end of the first month's intensive training Elie's instructor subjected him to a different type of test, this time in Jerusalem. He was given a French passport made out in the name of Marcel Cowen. (It actually belonged to an Egyptian-born Jew staying in Israel on his way to Africa. Elie's photograph had simply been substituted for that of the tourist while the test was in progress.)

He was handed the passport by Zeira, one of the secretaries at the Secret Service headquarters in Tel Aviv, and the Dervish gave him clear instructions: he was to go to Jerusalem and behave as if he were the real owner of the passport, who was known to speak only French and Arabic. In this role he was to contact as many persons as possible of his own choosing – tradesmen, employees, civil servants, even Ministers – who could give him information about Israel.

It was a typical "cover operation", to use the Secret Service jargon, and the Dervish coupled it with the exercise his new recruit had just completed at Tel Aviv. Cohen (alias Cowen) was told that throughout his stay in Jerusalem he would be followed by Secret Service agents; the more successfully he managed to dodge them, the better marks he would get.

He told his wife that he would be going to Jerusalem for a

43

few days on business. This time he had the excitement of behaving as if he were a spy in an enemy country. He travelled up by train and, as the temporary Marcel Cowen, registered in a small boarding-house, and then set out to see the town and make some suitable contacts.

He had been there only once before. The poorer quarters of Jerusalem, the little alleyways along the Jordanian frontier, the ancient wall separating the Israeli city from the Arab city, the Arab Legion firing-points ranged along the battlements – all this gave him the impression of being in an Eastern fortress. His assignment left him to his own devices, and gave him time for sightseeing and absorbing the city's unique atmosphere.

As he spoke fluent French, he had no difficulty in getting into conversation with some of his fellow-guests* at the boarding-house. He introduced himself as a tourist "from the south of France" and found them ready enough to tell him which cafés and restaurants were the best places for meeting businessmen and Government officials.

In this way, on his second day in Jerusalem, he made the acquaintance at the Café Vienna of a civil servant from one of the larger Ministries, who invited him home for dinner that evening. One of the dinner guests was the assistant manager of a small Jerusalem bank, who no sooner heard that the "French" tourist was planning to settle in Israel and transfer his modest capital there than he made an appointment with him for the next day at his office.

Thinking that he was on to a good thing, and hoping that his bank might have the benefit of this prospective capital, the assistant manager gave him a long and informative interview. Elie learned all about Israel's financial and economic problems, including the impending "catastrophe" when German repara-

---

* To avoid misunderstandings or embarrassment to various blameless citizens of Jerusalem, the authors prefer not to mention the names of the persons whom Elie Cohen got to know.

tion payments came to an end and the proceeds of American appeals fell off.

Cohen put innumerable questions to him, which were answered most politely and willingly. The young bank official must have been surprised, after all this, to hear nothing more of his customer.

The trainee spy realised that he was being followed in Jerusalem, as the Dervish had warned him he would be. Later he was able to see photographs taken of himself, including pictures of his meeting with the Ministry official at the Café Vienna. However, he managed to keep his interview with the banker secret, and his instructor complimented him on this.

"Operation Jerusalem" lasted for ten days, and Cohen (alias Cowen) got to know a remarkable number of business-men, officials and – Jerusalem being a university city – a few academics. His superiors were more than satisfied with the material he turned in; the Arab Secret Services would have been delighted to have it.

After going through the file, the Dervish drafted a report for the head of Mossad in which he stated that Elie was a remarkable personality; he had resource, original ideas and a knack of making contacts quickly. He also possessed initiative, imagination and quick mental reflexes, and was extremely good at inspiring confidence. Moreover, his mastery of several languages made his work easier. "I am therefore convinced," the Dervish concluded, "that he will succeed in the mission we are going to entrust to him, and that his desire to undertake it is wholly sincere. In addition, Cohen is obstinate, in the good sense: he is obstinately intent on his objective."

"Operation Jerusalem" had demonstrated that Elie was capable of assuming another person's identity and acting the part out permanently.

As a result the Dervish was convinced that when the time came, Elie could be planted in an Arab capital in the role of an

45

authentic Arab and not, as had been originally planned, as a Spaniard or South American. His appearance and his perfect accent in Arabic made such a project feasible, in the Dervish's judgment, with the minimum risk.

He had always had an excellent visual memory, and it was no problem for him to master the frequent and increasingly difficult exercises in memorising that the Dervish set him as part of his intensive training. Usually the lessons took place in the Allenby Street attic, where Yitzhak would spend hours exhibiting objects of all kinds on a table, covering these up after a few seconds, and then telling Elie to draw things he had hardly had time to glance at, or asking for details of this or that.

In the second phase of this exercise Elie was shown miniature models of different weapons, ranging from revolvers and rifles to various types of tank and supersonic aircraft. During the third stage he was shown slides of equipment actually available to Arab forces – the T 54 tank, the Mig 15, Mig 17, Mig 19 and even Mig 21, all aircraft of Soviet manufacture. The Dervish would tell Elie that the U.S.S.R. had not yet delivered them all to the Arab countries, but soon would. (Two years later the deliveries had been made.)

These exercises were continually repeated over and over again, for days and weeks. Yitzhak never got tired of insisting on the vital importance of an unerring visual memory; Elie must know the whole Arab arsenal by heart, almost automatically. The fewer written notes he took on enemy soil, and the more he relied on his memory, the better. "The place for written notes and files is at headquarters. All *you* need is your memory: that's essential."

By September 1960 Elie had earned his first leave, coinciding with Rosh Hashana, the Jewish New Year. It was practically the first opportunity he had had to play father to his tiny daughter, Sophie. He had lost his own father shortly after her birth.

His state of mind at this time is revealed by an otherwise unimportant episode. Ephraim Cohen, one of Elie's brothers, who lived in Kibbutz Revivim in the Negev, recalls his visit at the end of the summer. They called on a radio "ham" in the Kibbutz who had a private transmitter and was on the air to another amateur outside Israel. Elie seized the microphone and, to the amazement of his friends, shouted into it: "My name is Elie Cohen. I was thrown out of Egypt like thousands of other Jews. But there are still countless Jews in Egypt, all being ill-treated!"

His brother snatched the microphone back and spoke sharply to Elie: "Have you gone out of your mind? What's up with you?"

"The world must be told the truth," retorted Elie. "No one is doing a thing to help us."

This was the first and certainly the last time that Elie Cohen sent a message "in clear". He was to use a transmitter every day for years, but his future messages were to be in code and only a few people at Tel Aviv were in a position to decipher them.

7

A NEW IDENTITY

In the autumn of 1960, shortly after the Jewish New Year, Yitzhak the Dervish started building up Elie Cohen's new identity. It was a question, primarily, of turning a practising Jew into an equally conforming Moslem. For this purpose Elie was despatched to the Arab town of Nazareth under a false name in the guise of a student at the University of Jerusalem. His tutor was the patriarchal-looking Sheikh Mohammed Salmaan, who naturally had no idea of his pupil's real purpose or why he had so keen a hunger for Islam.

Squatting cross-legged on a carpet in the Sheikh's fine stone house, Elie settled down to assimilate the usages of the Moslem creed; he had started the study of its doctrines years ago in Alexandria. The bases of his instruction in ritual were the confession of faith, certain chapters in the Koran and, most important, the prayers for the different seasons and festivals. He learned by heart the five daily prayers and the famous "Fat'ha", the opening prayer that prefaces all the others.

He always carried on him a copy of the Koran, from which he learned passages by heart; the Sheikh complimented him on his rapid progress. On Fridays he would go to a mosque –

one finds them in Israel's Arab villages. There, with other worshippers, he would prostrate himself in the direction of Mecca, and would respond to the Muezzin's call to the faithful from the minaret: "There is no God but Allah, and Mohammed is his Prophet." 69-455

Elie's new identity would not require him to have a complete knowledge of Islam. It was essential to the success of his mission that he should appear to be an Arab "progressive" who had learned whatever he knew of religion in his childhood. But he was naturally assiduous, and so keen that he carried his studies far beyond the stage that his superiors expected of him.

In November the Dervish had another talk with him in the attic at Tel Aviv. "From today, you must start getting used to your new name – Kamal Amin Taabes. Kamal is your first name, Amin your father's name, Taabes your surname. Your family came from Syria originally."

Elie asked him if this was the best name he could think up; it wasn't a very attractive one.

"Not very attractive, but typically Syrian," said the Dervish, and he went on to point out that Elie was very lucky to have several months to get used to his name, whereas others, in similar circumstances often had to discover it from a forged passport handed them in the lavatory of an airport between flights.

He told him he was to be sent to Syria, and that he was now to spend the best part of his time making himself familiar with that country's geography, topography, history and economy up to date. "Above all", said the Dervish, "you will have to study the Syrian dialect and accent, which differ, as you know, from the Egyptian Arabic you speak."

(There are indeed distinct differences between the Arabic spoken in Damascus and that of Cairo. For instance, the "g" sound is hard in Egypt, but soft in Syria; thus, the Egyp-

49

tian President's name is pronounced Gamal Abdul Nasser in Egypt, but "Jamal" in Syria. There are also noticeable differences of vocabulary between the two countries.)

So after his lessons in dodging "shadows", in assuming a false identity and in the practices of Islam, Elie Cohen (now Kamal Amin Taabes) was given a teacher of Arabic phonetics who came originally from Damascus. He also had to tune in to Damascus Radio several times a day in order to acquire the Syrian accent and follow current events.

By now he had a very crowded programme, which began early in the morning and often lasted late into the night. Secret Service experts taught him to use various types of transmitter, ranging from everyday models to miniature devices that a spy could conceal. He was to work on his own in Syria, without any "ring"; so he followed all these courses alone and had solitary sessions with an instructor in the secret code he was to use later for his clandestine radio messages.

The courses in electronics that he had taken in Alexandria made the technical side of this training easy. His instructors were delighted to find that he had a light touch, with gentle pressure on the keys – a point of considerable importance later. Photographic gear which he had used as an amateur now became real professional equipment, and he learned, among other things to use a small camera to make microfilms.

Alone in a small projection room in Tel Aviv, he spent hours watching films on Syria. They included copies of Syrian television films, documentaries on life in that country and even secret shots of the Syrian armed forces and of military parades through the streets of Damascus.

At the same time, the future spy had to make a thorough study of the political situation in the country which he was to penetrate. He read through numerous pamphlets in Hebrew and Arabic, memorised a number of books, read and re-read newspapers, and learned by heart the dates and histories of key political episodes. And, of course, he followed current affairs in Syria every day.

As the Israelis saw it, the dominant political feature of 1960 was the mounting tension along the frontier with Syria. After the drubbing that Nasser's troops had received from General Moshe Dayan's Divisions during the Sinai Campaign, the frontier with Egypt had quietened down, but the temperature had risen by degrees along Israel's northern frontier. The brief Federal Union established just then between Syria and Egypt encouraged the Damascus Government to try to seize by force disputed strips of border territory.

Ben-Gurion, the Prime Minister of Israel, was sufficiently worried about the turn events might take in 1960 to make a detailed report to his Cabinet on January 17. In his view, Israel was involved against her will in a situation liable to become explosive overnight. With the increasing flow of modern arms from Russia and its satellites into the United Arab Republic – that is, into Egypt and Syria – he said the ratio of armed forces in the Middle East was constantly changing to Israel's disadvantage. He turned to the senior officer present from Military Intelligence (Modi'in), and asked him to give the exact figures of war material recently delivered to the U.A.R. adding that the general public in Israel unfortunately had no idea of what was going on in the nearby Arab capitals.

Israel, he concluded, must redouble her efforts to find further sources for the supply of arms and, at the same time, improve the flow of Intelligence, so as to forestall a possible military move from the direction of Damascus or Cairo. A fortnight later his warning was vindicated. The Syrians posted two Divisions of infantry and armour along the frontier at the southeast corner of the Sea of Galilee, with the object of preventing Israel from cultivating the borderland that formed part of the kibbutz of Tel Katzir (now renamed Beit Katzir).

Tension reached a climax when Syrian troops opened fire on this kibbutz and Mig 17 fighters made their first appearance over the Jordan valley. The Israeli Air Force at once sent up Super-Mystères obtained from France, and drove off the Syrian aircraft.

The Israeli general commanding the Northern Sector summoned a staff conference on January 31 to consider retaliatory measures, and announced that the Government was determined to preserve the *status quo* in this area at any cost. He exhibited at his headquarters fragments of Soviet shells that had been fired by Syrian artillery at the kibbutz that morning, and commented: "The Syrians have refused ever since 1957 to recognise the international frontier between our two countries, and are supported in this by Egypt. We do recognise this frontier and, if need be, we shall use our artillery to defend the original demarcation."

Two hours later an Israeli was killed and two men were injured, when Syrian guns opened up again on the target of Tel Katzir. That night (January 31–February 1) the Israeli Army struck back, and despatched its first punitive expedition since the Sinai campaign – this time into Syrian territory. Just before midnight the Golani Brigade began moving against the Syrian positions around Khirbet Tawafik, from which Tel Katzir had been shelled. The whole valley of the Jordan echoed to the din of exploding shells and automatic weapon fire.

The Syrians lit up the scene with powerful searchlights, but the Golani Brigade were too much for them, storming the fortified positions at Khirbet Tawafik and demolishing them. They blew up 50 houses and withdrew, leaving scores of Syrian troops dead. They brought back from the battlefield a considerable haul of armoured vehicles and light and heavy weapons of all kinds.

Elie Cohen was among the first to be shown the booty and to examine the various captured weapons. Under his instructor's guidance he was able to draw deductions from this battle. The Syrians, who were considered the best soldiers among the Arabs, had fought bravely, but had not been able to stand up to the better-trained Golani Brigade. The Dervish explained that victory at Khirbet Tawafik had been made possible because Tsahal* knew precisely what arms and men the Syrians had concentrated in this area.

"This information," he said, "enabled us to capture the positions in less than four hours. As a start we put the Syrian artillery out of action by accurate fire, based on exact knowledge of where the guns were sited. Briefly, the Syrians were able to shell Tel Katzir only as long as we allowed them."

The Dervish wanted Elie, while he was still on the Israeli side of the frontier, to draw the moral. "Victories like this", he pointed out, "can be won again and again, provided we can get the most accurate, relevant and speedy information on Syrian weapons, on the units stationed along our frontier, on the precise position of fortified posts, and on the movements of reinforcements. To get this information is vital, and it will be your job, once you are across the border, to provide it."

Cohen, who was spending that night in an Israeli outpost with the Dervish, had a sudden urge to cross the frontier there and then, and make for Damascus. He did not yet know that he would have to travel half-way round the world and back again before he would try out his luck in the streets, the Ministries and the military headquarters of that city.

He was soon to learn a good deal about the workings of the Intelligence Service of the United Arab Republic. Only a

* Hebrew abbreviation for Tsva Hagana L'Yisrael – Israel Defence Army (I.D.F.).

week after the Tawafik battle, the Israeli Under-Secretary for Defence, Shimon Peres, announced that appeals to several foreign Powers to supply Israel with the tanks and heavy weapons needed for her defence had met only with refusals. None of these countries was prepared to heed the Israeli warning that the United Arab Republic now had more tanks than Rommel and Montgomery had had between them during the Desert Campaign. France, still friendly to the Jewish State, was providing aircraft. All the other Powers declined to give Israel the arms she needed.

Meanwhile, the Joint Staff of the U.A.R. retained control of the situation and continued to direct Syrian troop movements against the northern frontier of Israel. On February 13 Nasser paid a surprise visit to Damascus; for security reasons his departure from Cairo had been kept secret, and his arrival in Syria was not announced until his aircraft had landed.

(No doubt he remembered the mysterious sabotage incident on this route at the start of the Sinai operation: at dawn on October 29, 1956, a Soviet-made Ilyushin with half the Egyptian General Staff on board had plunged into the Mediterranean somewhere off the coast of Israel, on its way back to Cairo from Damascus.)

Shortly after Nasser's visit to Damascus it came to the knowledge of Israeli Intelligence that open war between Israel and the U.A.R. had been on the verge of breaking out while he was there. They found out that their opposite numbers on the Egyptian and Syrian side had dreamed up an entirely imaginary Israeli troop concentration on the Syrian frontier. Untrue reports had filtered through from Arab observers in the border zone, to the effect that Israel was more than probably getting ready to invade Syria at any moment. These stories had been deliberately inflated, with every assistance from the celebrated Oriental imagination, as the rumours were relayed from the front to Headquarters in Cairo.

At the same time, Israeli Intelligence was astonished to discover another fact of unusual interest: the *Soviet* espionage service, having totally failed in 1956 to foresee the Sinai expedition, was anxious to prove for once that it was awake. So it was the first to warn the U.A.R. that Israel "was massing troops all along the Syrian frontier".

The Arab Intelligence Services fell into the Soviet trap. They were quick to blow up this information to the point of warning President Nasser that Israel was preparing to attack Syria. In so doing, they played into the hands of the Soviet leaders, who were perfectly aware that their "information" was a complete fabrication, but had put it about in Damascus and Cairo in order to throw the Arab leaders into a panic and, indirectly, remind them that in the event of danger their only hope of military and political support lay in Moscow.

These tactics soon bore fruit. What had begun as a Soviet "poisoning of the wells" was exploited and exaggerated for purely political purposes by the Arab Intelligence Services, and resulted in the U.A.R. working itself into a real state of alert. Neither in the West nor in the Communist countries was it realised that these moves, instigated by Moscow, had almost touched off an explosion, and threatened to set a full-scale Israel–Arab war ablaze in February 1960.

Having been briefed in Damascus on the supposed crisis, Nasser issued immediate orders for the Armoured Divisions stationed west of the Suez Canal to move quietly towards Gaza and the southern frontier of Israel. So 400 heavy tanks of recent Soviet manufacture crossed the Canal and passed rapidly through the Sinai Desert during the night of February 24/25. The Egyptian Army had learnt its lesson in 1956, and kept wireless silence as the armada of tanks moved up to the Israeli frontier. The Egyptians were convinced that this vast transfer of armoured units had not been noticed by the enemy.

But Israel had already learnt the news while the tanks

were crossing the Canal. The alert had been given by an Israeli reconnaissance aircraft, which supplied the Staff with remarkable high-altitude photographs, showing in detail the mighty columns of tanks crossing the desert.

When the Egyptian forces, which included T 34 and T 54 Soviet tanks and S.U. 100 anti-tank guns, as well as three Infantry Divisions, took up their positions in the desert near the Gaza sector of the frontier, they were startled to find a strong concentration of Israeli troops opposite them, equally arrayed for action.

All the same, it was the first time that Israel had been in the agonising situation of facing major enemy concentrations both to the north and to the south, Syrians as well as Egyptians. It was still more serious that these troops, facing Israel from either direction, were under a single command. Plainly, in such explosive conditions the slightest incautious or ill-advised move could bring on a war which in fact neither side really wanted.

The Government of Israel, having made the military dispositions required to face the double threat, decided that war at this juncture was to be avoided. This meant that Damascus and Cairo must be convinced that they had been led astray by their Intelligence Services and their deliberate distortion of the originally faulty and tendentious information supplied by Soviet Intelligence.

Accordingly, David Ben-Gurion, the Israeli Prime Minister and Minister of Defence, took the bold decision to behave as if this artificially-created border tension left him unmoved. Accompanied by the Israeli Chief of Staff, General Hayim Laskov, he left Jerusalem for Tel Aviv, where they attended a gala performance by Marcel Marceau, the French mime. Two days later he announced that he was off the following week on a visit to Canada and the United States.

Ben-Gurion's attitude of unconcern was effective. The tension melted away like a soap-bubble. The Egyptian Army withdrew from Sinai and recrossed the Suez Canal. Only the Syrians left strong forces in position on the Israeli border, proclaiming without conviction that they were going to launch a "Holy War against Israel".

An appreciation of this "clash of arms that never was" was given to Elie Cohen as part of his military and strategic training. Among its points were these:

(a) Syria has become the spearhead of Arab aggression against Israel. All information of any kind on internal developments in Syria is of vital importance to Israel;

(b) Absolute priority must be given to all information about possible operational plans directed against Israel;

(c) The effectiveness and reliability of the Intelligence Service necessarily require that all information transmitted shall be definite and accurate.

8

PASSENGER TO BUENOS AIRES

By the end of 1960 the decision had been taken to despatch Elie Cohen abroad – first of all to Buenos Aires, to establish the character of Kamal Amin Taabes. In view of his brilliant record as a trainee spy and the unsuspected resources he had revealed since his first meeting with the Dervish, the senior members of the Secret Service in Tel Aviv had made up their minds, first, that Cohen should be planted in Syria on a long-term basis and, secondly, that he must have a "cover story" that would allow him, when the time came, to get himself accepted by the ruling group in Damascus.

Once the decision was taken, his general training came to an end. During the two months before he left he concentrated on two tasks no less demanding than his previous labours. He had to study in depth the personality of the imaginary Kamal Amin Taabes: at the same time he must absorb the main features of the countries where he was to live, starting with Argentina.

The Dervish presented him with a file, in which the background of Kamal Amin Taabes had been expertly worked out in minute detail. In outline it went like this:

Kamal's father, Amin Taabes, had left Syria with his

wife, Saida (née Ibrahim) for Beirut, in the hope of making a better living there than at Damascus. Their son, Kamal Amin Taabes, was born in Beirut in 1930 (which made him six years younger than the genuine Elie Cohen), so he knew nothing about Damascus or Syria beyond what he had heard from his father or learnt at school. However, the elder Taabes had brought up his son to love Syria and look upon it as his own country. He himself had retained his Syrian nationality over the years, and had urged his son to go back there one day, once he had made his fortune abroad; he should then serve his country by joining the Syrian Nationalists in their patriotic struggle.

Kamal Amin Taabes had had an elder sister, who died in 1933, the year in which the Taabes family, including the three-year-old Kamal, left Beirut for Alexandria. Kamal had no personal recollection of Beirut, but was quite familiar with the Egyptian city to which his parents had migrated.

They had remained in Alexandria, where Amin Taabes had run a small textile business, till 1947. However, one of his brothers, who had migrated to Argentina a year earlier, kept bombarding his relatives in Alexandria with letters pressing them to come and "make their fortunes". So in 1947 Amin Taabes moved on again with his family to Buenos Aires. The two brothers, with a third partner, started a textile business there in Lebazi Street, which went bankrupt some years later.

Kamal had lost his mother in 1956, and his father six months later. After living for some time with his uncle and working for the Maradi travel agency he had eventually become the owner of a fair-sized import–export firm. How he had brought it to prosperity Cohen was to work out in detail on the spot.

The life-story of the Syrian expatriate Kamal Amin Taabes, evolved by the Secret Service at Tel Aviv, was basically simple enough; it was to a large extent tailored to fit the real history of the impersonator, who had no acquaintance with

Damascus or Beirut, but had indeed spent his youth in Alexandria and knew it like the back of his hand. But this personal history required him to be equally knowledgeable about Buenos Aires, where Kamal was supposed to have been living since he was 17.

He had to learn off by heart the contents of the detailed biographical file he was given at Tel Aviv. The Secret Service had, with great ingenuity, provided him with a "family album" – a minor masterpiece in its way – containing faked photographs illustrating the life of the Taabes family, with snapshots of Elie superimposed on a Buenos Aires background, alongside his "father", "mother" and "uncle". Nothing had been neglected that could substantiate the imaginary personality of Kamal Taabes and adorn it with realistic and concrete details.

Cohen spoke passable Spanish, but it was not good enough for someone who had lived so long in Argentina. So he devoted the last weeks before he left to an intensive finishing course in the language.

By the end of his training he had become identified with his new personality to such an extent that he found it hard to be his genuine self when he saw his wife at night in their flat at Bat Yam. Sometimes he even failed to answer to the name of Elie when she or his friends spoke to him.

On one occasion he was moved to confide in his instructor his anxiety lest his relations with his wife should suffer. "In my home", he said, "I make every effort to forget that I'm now Kamal Taabes. I ought to be able to keep my two identities entirely separate in my mind, but it isn't easy. Most of the day I have to behave like Kamal Taabes. How can I change back to Elie Cohen during the few hours I spent at home? It's really very difficult!"

Much later he was astonished to hear from his wife that even before he left for Argentina she had gathered practically everything. Feminine intuition told her that her husband was changing appreciably, and that the coming journey abroad, about which he had warned her, would take him "behind some mysterious curtain". Like any other Israeli wife in the same circumstances, she guessed that it was a secret mission involving the country's security, and she asked no needless questions.

The choice of Buenos Aires for Elie's first posting was no accident. It was designed to make his long-term mission in Syria easier. For some half-million Arab immigrants, including thousands of families from Syria, live in Buenos Aires, and the Secret Service at Tel Aviv reckoned on Cohen-Taabes finding people among them who could provide him with the political contacts he would need in Damascus.

Like other expatriate groups, the Arab community in Buenos Aires formed its own societies and clubs; "communal circles" for local Syrians had been started, much like Jewish "communal circles" in the United States or European countries. Alongside the Arab minority in Buenos Aires there is a substantial Jewish colony, most of whose members come from Europe, though there are a certain number of Jews from the Middle East among them. Some Jewish families who had been thrown out of Egypt, Syria or other Arab States, or had left these countries for fear of anti-Jewish discrimination, preferred to settle in South America rather than Israel.

Though Argentina has absorbed immigrants on such a large scale and of such varied origins, the various minorities tend to keep their individual identities. It is noticeable, for instance, that Arabs and Jews, especially in Buenos Aires, retain their national identity, speak little Spanish, and refuse to fall in with South American ways. Nor are they alone in this.

Legislation has been passed in Argentina to try to counteract this tendency. Every provision is made to facilitate the absorption and assimilation of newcomers; thus the

61

Argentinian passport conveys no information on the country of origin or religion of its holder. This fact is of incalculable value to all kinds of individuals who have an interest in discreetly leaving their native lands and disappearing from view in Argentina, where they acquire a new identity!

Why the Israeli Secret Service fixed on Buenos Aires can, then, be readily understood. Elie Cohen could turn up here under a false identity with a good chance that his arrival would arouse no immediate interest among his Syrian "compatriots". However, it was plain that despite all the facilities for absorption that Buenos Aires offered, the Israeli agent would have more than one branch of the Arab Counter-espionage to face there.

Arab embassies in Latin-American countries provide cover for a multiplicity of espionage and counter-espionage agents, and maintain special anti-Israeli propaganda departments designed to counterbalance the effective pro-Israeli propaganda coming from influential Jewish circles. Syrian Intelligence was known to be particularly active among the Arab colony of Buenos Aires.

A recent example shows the thoroughness with which Arab counter-espionage acts to attain its purposes in Argentina. It illustrates strikingly the way in which the secret war between Israeli and Arab agents is sometimes extended to areas very remote from the Middle East.

On January 17, 1964 an aircraft with the markings of the Egyptian Air Force landed at 10.37 on a military airfield in the south of Israel. Out of this Yak 11 (of Soviet manufacture) stepped an Egyptian pilot wearing a captain's insignia, who told the startled Israeli airmen, who rushed to the spot where he landed, that he was a deserter from the Egyptian Air Force and was seeking asylum in Israel.

The 26-year-old Mahmoud Hilmi had brought off an

extraordinarily bold coup. He had taken off that morning from the Bilbess military airfield, west of the Suez Canal, having filled his fuel tank as if for a training flight – he was an instructor – and crossed the Sinai Desert, to land on the first Israeli airstrip that he could spot from the air. Several Egyptian Mig fighters had given chase, but he had crossed the Israeli border unscathed. The whole operation had lasted a quarter of an hour.

One can easily imagine the welcome that this first deserter from the Egyptian Air Force received from the Israeli Air Force commander. At a press conference attended by Israeli and foreign journalists, and by officers from the station, Captain Hilmi explained that he had left Egypt for political and moral reasons.

For weeks he had taken part in Egyptian air raids on villages in the Yemen, as one of the operations in the war Egypt was waging against the Yemeni Royalists. Hilmi had decided to desert after being made to use gas on Yemeni villages. Since he belonged to a unit that was to conduct further raids on the Yemen, he had preferred to take refuge in Israel.

Captain Hilmi's flight from Egypt and his statements to the world press dealt the régime a psychological and moral blow that resounded like a thunderclap. It demonstrated, if demonstration was necessary, just how President Nasser contemplated establishing "revolutionary" order in a neighbouring country which resisted revolution. Hilmi's action also gave valuable evidence of the feelings of some sections of the Egyptian officer corps.

One can assume that the very day Hilmi escaped, the Egyptian authorities swore to avenge the damage he had done them. They had their chance much sooner than they could have dared to hope, and they were merciless.

Mahoud Hilmi spent nearly six months in Israel. Fêted and made much of by Israeli airmen, he lunched more than once with the Commander-in-Chief of the Israeli Air Force, at that

63

time General Ezer Weizmann. But as the months passed he expressed a wish to emigrate discreetly to Argentina. The Israeli authorities offered no objection, and he was provided with the necessary identity papers. They even found him a decent civil aviation job connected with agricultural projects not far from Buenos Aires; at 1,000 dollars a month, it would be fine for a bachelor.

Hilmi left Israel by air in June 1964. Unfortunately, despite repeated warnings from the Israeli Secret Service, he made two irreparable blunders, the first on his way to Argentina, and the second on his arrival in Buenos Aires under a false identity.

No sooner had his aircraft touched down at the airport of a European capital than he rushed to the transit lounge to send a postcard to his mother in Cairo. From this thoughtless action the Egyptian Secret Service easily deduced that Hilmi had left Israel.

On arrival in Buenos Aires, where he was to spend some days, he registered at a hotel. But the next day he decided to treat himself to a good meal at one of the countless Arab restaurants in the city, and met an Egyptian prostitute. He ought to have been more careful. Instead, he made the fatal mistake of telling her who he really was during the night, and how he had escaped to Israel.

Hilmi never returned to his hotel. His belongings and identification papers were left there.

A few days later, at the beginning of July, Mr. Levi Eshkol, the Israeli Prime Minister, arrived in Paris for discussions with President de Gaulle. At Orly, before he had left the V.I.P. lounge, he was handed a despatch from the Israeli Intelligence Service: Hilmi had disappeared, no doubt kidnapped by Egyptian agents in Argentina.

Mr. Eshkol ordered an immediate inquiry to see if the officials who had been dealing with Hilmi's problems had not

blundered or been careless. The upshot of this inquiry, passed on
to him in due course, was negative. The Israeli Secret Service
had not slipped up in any respect. Hilmi alone could be blamed
for his unhappy fate. The report observed that the Egyptian
Secret Service could not have been speedier or more efficient.
The very night that Hilmi misguidedly picked up his Egyptian
"hostess" Egyptian agents seized him and placed him in confine-
ment in the Embassy of the U.A.R.

Operation "Return to Cairo" – moved to bring the
deserter back to Egypt – took ten days. Hilmi was put aboard
an Egyptian vessel that had anchored off a port in Argentina,
and was put ashore in Alexandria. Two months later it was
learnt that he had been secretly court-martialled for desertion
and high treason, condemned to death and executed in Cairo.

The activity of Arab agents in Argentina did not pass
unnoticed by the Israelis. Elie Cohen's departure was therefore
planned with care and strict precautions were taken over his
journey, which involved a few days' stop in Europe. All his
arrangements were made, and when the time came, Cohen said
good-bye to his wife and daughter and the rest of his family,
promising to be back soon from his "business" trip abroad. He
said he would write as often as he could, and kept his word.
Nadia received news of him, though never from Argentina: his
letters always had a European postmark.

Elie Cohen, the anti-James Bond, was driven to Lydda
airport by a boy called Gideon in a plain van belonging to the
Secret Service. He had with him a small suitcase which had seen
some wear, a passport in his own name, and an envelope containing 500 dollars that Gideon had handed to him. Going
through the Israeli customs, he boarded an El Al airliner for
Zurich. When he got there he was, according to instructions
from the Dervish, to take the airport bus to the town terminal,

65

where he would be looked after by an agent whose name and appearance he knew absolutely nothing about.

Everything went off according to plan. He took the bus to the terminal on the Bahnhofstrasse, where he was greeted by a well-dressed middle-aged man who spoke Hebrew with a slight German accent. He introduced himself as Israel Salinger and drove him to his hotel, near the Lake.

During his three days in Zurich Cohen spent several hours each day with Salinger, who was "Resident Director" of the Israeli Secret Service in Europe. He had a good front as manager of a large import–export firm, and his immediate job was to give Cohen some elementary business briefing. In Buenos Aires Cohen-Taabes would ostensibly be running a business that arranged the transport of goods by sea and air, for which the agent for Europe (and Zurich in particular) was Salinger. Cohen therefore had to know, at least in outline, how such a concern functioned, and should be particularly familiar with the vocabulary of the freight business.

Salinger gave Cohen a cheque-book from a well-known Zurich bank, where an account had been opened in the name of Kamal Amin Taabes. "Every South American businessman", he explained, "has his Swiss bank account".

On Elie's last day in Zurich they went shopping in the Bahnhofstrasse, and he acquired a complete wardrobe with Swiss markings, including a suit, an overcoat, two pairs of shoes, and some ties and handkerchiefs.

Finally, at the hotel, Elie handed his Israeli documents and clothes to Salinger, keeping nothing which could indicate what country he had come from. He collected a South American passport in the name of Taabes and his airline ticket for Buenos Aires, repacked his bag with the clothing bought in Zurich and, after Salinger had given him a box-number in Zurich where he could address mail to be forwarded to Nadia, he left for the air-port alone. He was now officially Kamal Amin Taabes. The

plane took him to Paris, where he made a transit stop of a few
hours at Orly airport, and resumed his journey to Argentina.
Months later he told the Dervish that throughout the long
flight across the Atlantic he could not get the kidnapping of
Eichmann out of his mind.

Cohen had just enrolled in the Israeli Secret Service at
the time of the Eichmann incident, and he had gained the
confidence of his senior colleagues to such an extent that before
he left Tel Aviv he had been invited to a meeting of a few select
members of the Service, where they were given a detailed
account of how the operation had been carried out in Buenos
Aires a short while before. (These details have still not been
published in Israel or elsewhere. So far only a few innocuous
scraps of information, largely inaccurate and incomplete, have
been pieced together from various sources.)

As he flew towards Buenos Aires, Cohen recalled various
details of the kidnapping. It occurred to him his own journey
was exactly the reverse of Eichmann's, though Eichmann had
known nothing about it. (He had been drugged in the El Al
aircraft transporting him and his escort of Israeli Secret Service
agents from Buenos Aires to Lydda.)

"The story of that kidnapping," Cohen later told the
Dervish, "filled me with courage. It made me realise that our
Service could carry out the most difficult operations. So I felt
more confident as I was being flown off in the opposite direction."

Even at Buenos Aires airport he glanced at the planes on
the runways, trying to reconstruct the take-off of the El Al
machine which had carried the Secret Service's prize catch back
to Israel.

There was no one to meet him, and there was no trouble
with the passport and customs inspection. Carrying his suitcase
and his passport in the name of Taabes, he made for the Tourist

Information Bureau and was given the address of a suitable hotel. He took a taxi there – it was a medium-category establishment in the Avenida Nuevo de Julio (Ninth of July Avenue), the main thoroughfare of Buenos Aires – and booked a room with bath for a week.

The night that he arrived – early in February 1961 – the smart avenue, built by President Peron on the model of the Champs-Elysées, was thick with people and sparkling with hundreds of neon signs. Kamal Amin Taabes took his first stroll; he must make every effort to enter into the spirit of this great city, where he was to create a new character for himself and clear the way for his ultimate move into Syria.

Next day he had an initial, highly secret meeting with a local contact. Salinger had told him that he should go to the Café Corintas on the Avenida Nuevo de Julio at eleven in the morning, and had warned him that this meeting, though essential, should be as brief as possible. Plainly any conceivable risk of being shadowed by Egyptian or Syrian agents was to be avoided.

Just as in Zurich, he had not been told anything about the person he was to meet. However, he was at the Café Corintas just before eleven, and settled down at a table and ordered a drink. A few moments later a man of about 65 with a shock of white hair came up and shook hands, introducing himself as "Abraham". Like Salinger, he had identified Cohen-Taabes from a photograph supplied by the Secret Service at Tel Aviv. They had only a brief conversation, in Spanish. No one in that large and crowded café had any idea that one of the major espionage operations of the century had just been launched before their very eyes.

After a few words of welcome, Abraham passed across a newspaper on which he had scribbled an address where Cohen could rent a well-furnished flat. Then he gave him by word of mouth the address of a Spanish teacher, telling him frankly that his Spanish accent was poor and he would do well to take lessons.

It was arranged that Abraham should contact Cohen from time to time, though as seldom as possible. In extreme urgency he could be reached at a certain telephone number. Another address and telephone number that Elie was to memorise was that of his supposed sea-and-air freight firm, where there would always be someone to answer calls and confirm that Mr. Taabes really was the owner and managing director. Abraham undertook to provide visiting cards and headed paper by the following day. Within three months he was also to obtain for him an Argentinian passport in the name of Taabes.

At the end of this first meeting he handed over a folded sheet of paper listing the names and addresses of prominent local Arabs and particulars of the Islam Club of Buenos Aires and the Arab restaurants favoured by Syrian and Lebanese expatriates.

"Get in touch with these people as soon as you can," he added, "And you'll get letters of introduction for Damascus." He shook hands again and left the table, but came back as if he had just remembered something. Bending down he whispered in Hebrew "Behatslaha" ("Good Luck").

Elie Cohen, from that day, enjoyed a series of successes brought about by a combination of good luck, coincidence and presence of mind. Before February was out he had made the acquaintance of an important character who, without realising the fact, was to set him on the road to Damascus.

Within his first week, he had become a familiar figure in the Islam Club recommended to him by Abraham. In his role of Kamal Amin Taabes he had no difficulty in joining, and he passed hours every day in the club reading the Cairo and Damascus newspapers provided.

F

He got into conversation – in Arabic, naturally – with young immigrants from Lebanon and Syria, frequently joined them in games of Shesh-Besh (the Middle Eastern name for backgammon which is a national pastime in every Arab country), and ate a late supper with them, as people do in Buenos Aires. Without saying much, he dropped a few discreet hints from time to time about his life and character.

He took care to let them know, among other things, that he was a businessman who had amassed a modest fortune, and that his dearest wish was to go back to his parents' native land and play an active part in public life. He and his fellow-members would spend much of the night talking about the current problems of Syria.

One day a chair at the table where he was playing Shesh-Besh was occupied by a man in his fifties who was held in high respect in Arab society in Argentina – Abdullah Latif Alheshan. Rather short and somewhat portly, with a fine moustache, but going bald, he was the vigorous editor-in-chief of the leading Arab weekly in Buenos Aires, *Al Alam al Arabi* ("The Arab World").

Cohen-Taabes had noticed him the second time he was in the club, and had been waiting for a good opportunity to get to know him. Shesh-Besh provided an excellent cover. As he moved his pieces around, Taabes started a long conversation with Alheshan on the political situation in Syria, remarking that he was tired of living "in exile", that he considered himself Syrian, not Argentinian, and that he had a longing for his own country. "To be brief," he announced, in the most natural way in the world, "I'm planning to leave for Damascus very soon."

Alheshan was delighted to hear this. He invited Taabes to visit his newspaper office and continue their talk. Taabes accepted with alacrity, and they immediately fixed an appointment for February 23. This date clearly shows Cohen's rate of progress and how rapidly he had managed to insinuate himself into influential circles in Buenos Aires. Barely a fortnight after his arrival in Argentina – a foreign country which was completely strange to him – he was sitting in a comfortable armchair talking to the editor of the Arab weekly of Buenos Aires.

They went on chatting for more than two hours, and this was only the first of a long series of meetings between them. The journalist questioned the young "Arab" about his life and his family, and Taabes produced an inexhaustible flow of anecdotes about his younger days, about Alexandria, about his parents' move from country to country, and about his business in Buenos Aires.

Taabes deduced from some of Alheshan's remarks that he would have liked to see the "Baath" (Rebirth) party of Syria take over the Government. Moreover, Alheshan told him bluntly that while he favoured co-operation between Syria and Nasser's Egypt, he was opposed to Egyptian annexation of the "Province of Syria" and took exception to the way in which Nasser's administration of Syria was exploiting the country.

This gave Cohen-Taabes an opening. "I'd be prepared (he said) to leave for Syria this very day, to make my contribution towards the national effort. But I'm dubious about the reception I'd get. I don't know anyone in Damascus. I might be wasting my time and squandering all my good intentions."

Alheshan reassured him: "When you decide to go to Damascus, don't hesitate to call on me. I'll give you introductions to all my friends; don't worry. In the meantime, come and see me again as often as you like. I like you, and you can consider me your friend."

Before they separated, Alheshan asked Taabes for his address, so that he could send him the weekly he edited. Taabes gave him the address of the flat he had just rented in Buenos Aires, 1485 Taquarra Street; he also handed him a visiting card with the name and address of his firm.

He felt that he had won the journalist's confidence, and

so he had – more than he knew. Four years later, when Elie Cohen was sentenced to death in Damascus, Alheshan produced some concrete evidence by sending an open letter to the most important Arab daily in the Middle East, *El Hayat* in Beirut. In reply to allegations made in Damascus, accusing him of giving invaluable assistance to the Israeli spy, he wrote:

> *One day a young man of about 30, with fair skin and black hair, called on me and introduced himself as Kamal Amin Taabes. He told me he had spent his youth in Egypt. I often ran across him at receptions and cocktail parties at Arab embassies and at the Islam Club, where all the young Arabs of Buenos Aires congregate. We had a number of conversations. He was usually rather reserved, and gave the impression of being a serious and thoughtful young man. He took a keen interest in the problems of the Arab world, and asked me to pass the Arab newspapers on to him; after I had read them.*

In the course of his letter, Alheshan notes that one day Taabes told him he would be going back to Syria. "It is quite true that I gave him some letters of introduction. But it was not I who sent him to Syria to spy for Israel. He was granted the necessary visas to enable him to go to Damascus by his personal friends, the Consuls-general of the Arab states. If, after that, he managed to outwit all the Arab Secret Services for four years, why pick on me for not realising, after just a few conversations, who the man really was?"

Though Cohen himself did not realise, when he met Alheshan, how completely he had won his trust, his intuition told him that he had been successful in playing the part of Kamal Taabes, and that the character of Elie Cohen was now past history. He also knew that his local contact, Abraham, was effectively engaged in implementing his "cover story", and had provided all the evidence that might be required if his new acquaintances should start prying into his personal affairs and family history. He experienced the helpful influence of Abraham's "long arm", at every stage, and his confidence was reinforced by the knowledge that he had this backing and protection in his work.

From time to time he received from Abraham the funds he needed to maintain a standard of living sufficiently high for the part he was supposed to play. He had always been used to living modestly, and his expenses did not strain the resources of the Israeli Secret Service. Indeed, they fell rather below the normal budget.

What Abdullah Latif Alheshan wrote in his open letter four years later was true enough. Cohen-Taabes had certainly not been satisfied just to make contact with the editor-in-chief of the local Arab weekly. Within a few weeks, he had succeeded in becoming a regular guest at all the diplomatic receptions held by Arab representatives in Buenos Aires. He was to be seen at all Arab functions, most of them arranged by the Islam Club, and he attended the cocktail parties of the Arab embassies.

Within a few weeks he had become a kind of permanent, if unobtrusive, feature of the landscape on semi-social, semi-political occasions of this kind. This was a remarkable achievement in itself. Anyone familiar with diplomatic parties knows that there is nothing easier than to become a regular guest at such social gatherings, if one cares to do so. One just has to know one's way around, and have the nerve to turn up at the right time and place. Hosts and guests soon get used to seeing such people at every reception, without puzzling about who they are or why they are there.

All the same, Cohen's presence in all the Arab embassies had its unusual aspects. Having insinuated himself into this set, he still had to keep up the role of Kamal Taabes without slipping up and to extend the circle of his personal contacts in a way which would profit him later.

Among those whom he met in this way was the man who,

four years later, would confirm the death-sentence passed on him: General Amin el-Hafez, at that time Military Attaché in Buenos Aires. He was a handsome man, going grey, with a wisp of hair constantly straying down his forehead. He looked more like a South American than a Syrian.

Taabes was introduced to the General by Abdullah Alheshan, and the Attaché, resplendent in dress uniform, engaged them both in a long political discussion. He expressed full confidence in the future of the Baath party, to which he belonged, and claimed that it was the only party that could restore the country's glory. He told them that by the end of the year he would have completed his tour of duty in the Argentine, and that once he was back in Syria he would devote himself to political activity within his own party.

The dashing Military Attaché naturally could not know that the Baath party would soon raise him to the highest office in his country, the Presidency of the Syrian Arab Republic.

Taabes, listening closely, ventured only one comment: "If I were in Damascus, General, I should do the same."

"What are you waiting for, then?" said Amin el-Hafez. It sounded like an order. Then he turned away to speak to another guest.

Cohen-Taabes, in a later report to his superiors, observed that General el-Hafez had certainly taken in his comment, since on several occasions when they met, he had asked him, with a wink: "Well, when are you off to Syria?"

During his secret meetings with Abraham (which were infrequent, with a different rendezvous on each occasion), Cohen would pass over detailed reports on his constantly-developing connections with Arab circles. Abraham was pleased with him and handed him, at the end of three months, the promised Argentinian passport and identity card in the name of Kamal Amin Taabes. In May he gave him fresh instructions from Tel Aviv: Cohen was to tell his friends that he had decided to leave quite soon for a tour of the Arab countries, and that he intended to visit Damascus and investigate the prospects of settling there permanently.

Taabes lost no time. He made the round of his acquaintances to extract the promised introductions. Abdullah Alheshan was as good as his word. When Taabes called on him on May 13 and told him he had made up his mind to go and would be glad of letters of introduction, he was delighted. He showed Taabes a letter he had just written to his son in Damascus, and added there and then a few lines introducing his friend Kamal Taabes. He also gave Taabes a separate letter commending him to his son, and three other letters in the same vein addressed to his friend Nabib Hareb (a well-known businessman in Damascus), a cousin in Alexandria, and a prominent banker at Beirut.

In this way Taabes collected from his Arab friends in Buenos Aires quite a batch of letters, most of them addressed to their relatives in Lebanon and Syria. He was careful to assure everyone that he was going on a tour of several Arab capitals, but would also break his journey in Europe.

It was no problem to obtain an Egyptian visa from the U.A.R. Embassy in Buenos Aires, and the Lebanese consulate gave him a visa valid for six months. Cohen-Taabes was therefor ready to start on his journey, with Damascus as his final destination. Six months had passed since he had landed in Argentina, and his new identity was firmly established.

At the end of August he left Buenos Aires on a flight to Zurich, going this time via London, where he did not stay. Acting on instructions sent him through Abraham, he simply changed planes at Zurich, and went on this time to Munich. Passing through the customs and passport control, he recognised an old acquaintance at Munich airport – Israel Salinger, his "Resident Director" in Europe.

Throughout Cohen's stay in Argentina Salinger had dutifully forwarded his letters – addressed to a box-number in

75

Zurich – to Nadia in Israel, naturally mailing each one from a different European city. Cohen's letters to his wife were short, and simply spoke of the "business" complications that were keeping him busy in Europe. While he was abroad, his monthly salary was paid to Nadia through a fictitious commercial firm.

Cohen gave Salinger a detailed account of his work in Argentina, and said, more than once, that he felt perfectly ready to leave for Damascus, and would gladly do so that very day. However, the last directive that Salinger passed on told Cohen that he was not to go there for several months. For the present he was to return to Tel Aviv for a final training course.

Cohen handed over to Salinger his identity documents in the name of Taabes, and the letters of introduction for the Arab capitals, as well as the clothes he had got in Argentina. He got back from him his Israeli identity documents and the original clothes left with him in Zurich. In the spare time he had in Munich he went shopping for presents for his wife, his small daughter and the rest of his family. Finally, he took off in an Israeli airliner for Tel Aviv.

At Lydda airport he was welcomed back by the same Mossad commercial van driven by Gideon, who asked no questions, but took him straight to Bat Yam. His return was as much of a surprise to his family as his departure had been. After six months' absence, his wife and family were overjoyed to see him again. This was the first opportunity he had to teach little Sophie to call him "Abba", the Hebrew for "Daddy". He told the rest of them about his European trip; without a word about his stay in South America. He spent the first week of September alone with his family, undisturbed even by the Dervish.

9

INTERLUDE IN ISRAEL

Elie knew that the respite in Bat Yam, before he returned to his secret service work, would be a short one. His official instructor, Yitzhak, the "Dervish", brought the family holiday to a close by asking him out to lunch in Jaffa at the Restaurant Chez Jeannette, where excellent grilled fish is served. As they sat outside the restaurant, facing the old port, they could have been taken for a father and son having a chat on family matters. The Dervish was certainly paternal, but he was listening to his protégé's adventures in South America.

He remarked that Elie now had a Spanish accent even when he spoke Hebrew, to which Elie replied: "Just wait till you hear my Arabic; in Buenos Aires they always speak Arabic with a Spanish accent." He felt completely relaxed, and having told his tale, he expressed the conviction that he was well enough equipped with introductions to start on the job that was waiting for him. "I feel I can press on to Damascus now and get myself accepted among the top people."

Later, the Dervish noted in his report, that Cohen had such complete self-confidence that it was catching, and other senior members of the Secret Service in Tel Aviv who had had dealings with him while he was in Israel during September

1961 had much the same impression. This was certainly a positive and encouraging fact to register. Yet, from another point of view, over-confidence on the part of a secret agent can be dangerous for him, and can easily lead to thoughtless behaviour and taking excessive risks.

In any event, it was decided that Cohen should be put through one final course before they finally let him go, and meanwhile he was to write postcards, to be mailed from various Western capitals, to Arab friends of his in Buenos Aires, in case they were getting worried about him.

His only comment on the disappointing news from the Dervish was "I'd never have thought that the road to Damascus was so long; one could die of exhaustion and frustration before getting there." This was not so much a display of temper as the genuine restlessness of a war-horse sniffing the scent of the battlefield. However, his superiors were of another opinion. Further training was required, and the detailed plan for his mission in Syria had now to be formulated in the light of the remarkable outcome of his preliminary posting to Argentina.

So Elie found himself back once more in the Dervish's little attic in Allenby Street, learning from a specialist instructor in secret radio transmission how to handle the type of apparatus that he was to use in Damascus. He made rapid progress, and by the end of a few weeks succeeded in attaining speeds of 40 to 50 words a minute, which experts consider a decent average. He learned to use several secret codes, practised reading the cipher messages tapped out by his instructor, and got to know the codes by heart.

One point about this final stage of his training should be borne in mind. One of the duties of the radio instructor was to spot Elie's personal idiosyncrasies of touch while transmitting. To the expert, this varies from one individual to another and is as individually distinctive as a thumb-print.

In other words, the type of morse signals transmitted

from a station at a certain distance can establish the identity of the sender without any need for an explanatory preamble. The slightest variations in touch, modifications imperceptible to the untrained ear, are so many concrete indications, instantaneously registered and understood by the experienced operator who receives and deciphers.

Accordingly, a very limited number of radio operators of the Secret Service decipherment centre at Tel Aviv made it their business, from September 1961 onwards, to study Cohen's practice messages and distinguish them from others. These were the operators who listened for his messages from Damascus later on.

Part of his time was spent learning how to improvise different kinds of synthetic ink; how to devise hiding places for objects in a flat; how to conceal secret equipment in household utensils of every kind; how to carry firearms, documents, letters of microfilms sewn into clothing or next to the skin. He was going through the regular curriculum of a secret agent's apprenticeship. Contrary to the public image that certain spy thrillers have given it, Secret Service training demands a sustained effort, and has nothing exciting about it but the name.

Once more, he scrutinised miniature or full-size models of weapons used by the Syrian army, and had intensive practice in firing revolvers and German Schmeisser automatic rifles like those issued to Syrian troops. He was also taught to handle different types of explosive. During firing practice the Dervish kept insisting that he was not to shed a drop of blood in Damascus. "However," he added, "Syria is a republic on the South-American pattern, where the next revolution is apt to break out overnight. You might be obliged to use firearms in self-defence. But you will not do so except in dire emergency."

During these last three months of 1961 Elie listened to Damascus radio more attentively than ever before, and kept a close watch on political developments in Syria.

A decisive change occurred in Syria on September 28, 1961: the Union with Egypt was disrupted. It was as sudden and as startling as the formation of the United Arab Republic three years earlier. Syria regained her political and economic independence, and expelled her Egyptian "protectors". But having renounced her secondary status as "the Province of Syria" and part of the United Arab Republic, independent Syria was rent by a merciless struggle between political groups. The country became the battleground of an undeclared civil war in which the prize was power, but no one had in fact attained the power summit.

Nonetheless, it became clear that this country, which had witnessed twelve revolutions and *coups d'état* in thirteen years, was going to be dominated – and dominated for a long time – by the Baath party. Some of this party's more influential supporters had been friendly with Cohen in Buenos Aires, and he had actually sent to General Amin el-Hafez in Argentina that very month a postcard mailed from Zurich, with the simple words "Baath for ever!" above his signature.

He followed the crisis in Syria meticulously, and was given access to Tel Aviv's secret files. He was soon able to sort out the principal figures in the rising against Nasser. However, he and his superiors had to agree that, as far as the evidence showed, a move in any direction was possible in Syria: future developments were outside the scope of political analysis and remained absolutely unpredictable. Israeli Intelligence officers have a saying that in Syria "power goes to the officer who gets up in the morning earlier than his rivals and takes over the Radio Station".

The real master of Syria, and prime mover in the coup against Nasser, was a young Syrian colonel called Abdel Karim Nahalawi. As Military Assistant to Marshal Amer, and a trusted servant of Nasser, he had been appointed Deputy-Governor of the "Province of Syria".

The Colonel had, however, been planning for some time to free Syria from its commitment to Egypt. He had heard the rumblings of discontent from the peasant masses, and also from the middle classes who were the first to suffer from the Egyptian annexation of their country. Peasants and businessmen accused Egyptian officials of exploiting the rich natural resources of Syria and its greater prosperity. Syrian officers were aggrieved that Syrian units had been put under Egyptian commanders. The Syrian Military Air Training School had been transferred to Egypt, together with a squadron of Mig 17 aircraft supplied to Syria by Russia. Egyptians were even given top posts in the Syrian civil service.

Meanwhile, the Baath People's Party, run by an élite of young officers, had been muzzled. The political and economic principles of this party were an odd combination of Socialist theory and Nationalist practice. Still, it stood out as the only pan-Arab party with a clearly defined programme and relatively good organisation. Its popularity and the support it won from the "Young Turks"* of the Damascus military clique were bound to obstruct Nasser's plans for the "Province of Syria", and the party was inevitably and systemically gagged – which made the reawakening of the Baath, when the coup occurred on September 28, seem all the noisier.

The day Marshal Abdul Hakim Amer,† the Egyptian Governor of Syria, received news in the small hours of the morning, while he was still in bed, that Colonel Nahalawi had seized the radio station and proclaimed to the people of Syria that Union with Egypt was over. The Marshal at once telephoned to Cairo and spoke to President Nasser, who said he was ready to come to Damascus immediately and re-establish order.

---

* i.e. militant reformers.

† Marshal Amer was President Nasser's Deputy and Commander-in-Chief of the Egyptian Army during the Six-Day War. He resigned after the war and either committed suicide or was murdered in September 1967 following the discovery of a plot against Nasser.

Nasser realised what a moral defeat the collapse of the Union with Syria would represent in the eyes of the world in general and the Arabs in particular. Even then, he enjoyed enormous personal prestige in Syria, and might have had a fair chance of regaining control.

However, Marshal Amer advised him against intervening personally, assuring him that he was perfectly capable of re-establishing law and order in Syria and restoring the *status quo*. But Brigadier Nahalawi and his men proved the stronger. During the morning the young Brigadier had Marshal Amer arrested and escorted to the aircraft that flew him back to Cairo. Two Egyptian paratroop commando units landed in the Syrian port of Latakia, where they enjoyed the protection of Egyptian destroyers anchored in the harbour; but they surrendered without a shot being fired. Colonel Nahalawi had within a few hours become the undisputed but almost unrecognised master of Syria. He set up a Government of experienced professional politicians.

The Syrian coup raised the temperature of the whole Middle East. The Israeli Government could not fail to rejoice at President Nasser's reverse; the collapse of the Union between Egypt and Syria had removed the danger of the two countries' forces being united under a single command. On the other hand, it also meant that Israel must expect another development of which she had more than once borne the brunt: the animosity between Damascus and Cairo was likely to result once more in each out-bidding the other in incitement against Israel, which would start with propaganda and develop into action.

For Elie Cohen's future work in Damascus the Egyptian expulsion from Syria was of capital importance. So long as the Union between the two countries was in force, his orders were to avoid contact with Egyptian circles at all costs. His superiors were naturally afraid of him being identified by some Egyptian from Alexandria. Worse – when we recall his arrest and interrogation by the Egyptian Security Service in 1954 – he might

run across an agent who had known him at that time in Alexandria or Cairo. The Egyptian withdrawal from Damascus
therefore cleared the horizon for him and made his future
operations there to some extent easier.

As a result of the events of September 28 he was given a
further political directive. The Baath Party now had every
chance of seizing power, and in Buenos Aires Cohen had expressed personal sympathy for this party, openly and in the
presence of General Amin el-Hafez. He had even reaffirmed his
loyalty to the party in the postcard that the Dervish had got him
to send the General via Switzerland. Nonetheless, his superiors
made it clear that if he managed to penetrate influential Baath
circles in Damascus, he was still to avoid enrolling as a party
member. It was better to go slow and wait for the political
situation in Syria to clear. Until then one could not be sure
whether the Baath would stay on top; meanwhile, it would be
too risky for an Israeli agent to adopt any definite political
label.

A leading member of the Israeli Secret Service summed
up the situation for him in a rather graphic sentence: "If you're
rash enough to announce your support for the Baath too soon,
you risk being shot, not as an Israeli spy, but as a member of a
party that, after the next *coup d'état*, will probably be banned
and persecuted by the new Government."

Cohen's utter serenity – to the point of eccentricity,
even – in the face of the tumultuous developments in Syria,
where "Taabes" was so soon to appear, had been remarked on
by his superior officers. His Secret Service colleagues were struck
by his remarkable inner calm and by the way in which his
composure was reinforced by modesty. He followed the
sequence of events in Syria on the radio, on television and in the
newspapers, and analysed the situation as if he were getting
ready for a holiday in Damascus rather than a mission which
would expose him to every kind of danger. Yet he knew as well

as his senior colleagues that he was going to a country that surpassed all other Arab States in its virulent political fanaticism and its nationalist and militarist excesses.

The surprising assurance with which Cohen spoke of his future assignment, and his complete confidence in its success, prompted his superiors to tell him over and over again not to rush things once he got to Damascus, but to work his way gradually and progressively into the ruling circles of Syria.

His purpose would be to provide Tel Aviv with the maximum information in two spheres of prime importance. One was the Syrian Army, its organisation and strength, its manoeuvres inside the country and on the frontier with Israel, and every detail about its commanders and officers. "Whatever happens to the Damascus Government, and whatever the political situation," he was assured, "the Syrian Army will remain the dominant and decisive factor in the country's future for a long time."

Secondly, he was to provide information about the economic situation in Syria. He was urged not to waste time and energy on subjects of lesser urgency. As we shall see later, this injunction was more than once disregarded by his superiors themselves.

Information of capital importance, calling for immediate military or strategic reaction from Israel, was to be sent by Cohen with the utmost speed. He had for this purpose a miniature transmitter no bigger than a cigarette packet. This technical masterpiece, rarely used even by the espionage Services of great powers and almost unknown among the Secret Services of other nations, was to be handed over to Cohen later, on the Continent. A technical triumph, it was to be the channel for an inexhaustible flow of first-rate information on events in Syria; in Tel Aviv it was regarded as positively magical. For the time being he was supplied with a rather special electric razor, in which the flex was the antenna of the future transmitter. He was to use this for sending short messages – they had to be short to reduce the risk of detection by the Syrian Counter-Espionage Service.

Transmission times and even the date for sending the first message were fixed there and then. Cipher agreed on in advance would convey to Tel Aviv that Cohen had leased a flat and was properly fixed up there. Until he had the flat it was out of the question for him to communicate with Israel, even in an emergency. Another prearranged cipher would convey Tel Aviv's desire that he should leave for Europe at the first opportunity, and contact his "Resident Director", Salinger.

He was to leave at the end of December 1961, and once more he told his wife that "business" required him to spend some months in Europe. Nadia asked him to make his stay abroad as brief as possible. The same plain van, with the same driver, was waiting to drop him at Lydda airport for a flight to Munich, where he met Salinger again.

Changing his clothes once more, he left his Israeli outfit with Salinger and received in exchange the clothing he had worn in Argentina. Salinger also gave him back his Argentinian passport stamped with Egyptian and Lebanese visas. Only the most important visa – for Syria – was lacking; he was to get this in Zurich.

Salinger instructed him to buy a steamer ticket for Lebanon. They chose the liner *Astoria*, which was to leave for Beirut in the first week of January. Days before he left, Cohen had seen a passenger list obtained through rapid, but discreet, inquiries made by European contacts of the Israeli Secret Service.

He got from Salinger a small suitcase containing household appliances, the kind a bachelor might take with him from one continent to another. Among them was a medium-size electric mixer made of plastic, a normal commercial model with one difference: it had a double bottom fixed in it to conceal the miniature wireless set that Elie had studied and tried out in

Tel Aviv. In his Munich hotel room Salinger showed Cohen the false bottom, removed the tiny transmitter from it, and told him how to close the electric machine again and how to use it as a mixer once the transmitter had been extracted.

One minor incident in Munich the day after he got there demonstrated how satisfactorily Cohen's technical knowledge now equipped him for his duties. The night before, after Salinger had left him, Cohen had been practising with the mixer again, assembling and dismantling it, and had noticed that every time it was moved it made an odd noise. The tiny transmitter was badly lodged in its hiding place and rattled about inside the double bottom.

"Let me have the apparatus back at once, and I'll get it put right," said Salinger. Cohen said the job was already done. He had found out for himself how to remedy the fault, and the mixer now worked perfectly, both for preparing cocktails and for sending secret messages.

Leaving a short note for Nadia with Salinger, he was off by air next day to Zurich, where he went straight to the Syrian Consulate; the consul there made no difficulties about stamping a Syrian visa in Taabes's Argentinian passport. An Italian transit visa was forthcoming without any hold-up.

Cohen-Taabes spent New Year's Eve in Zurich, mingling with the cheerful crowds that surged through the streets from midnight till the small hours, but keeping to himself as he strolled through the city. His thoughts were thousands of miles away in an enemy country whose frontier he would cross a few days hence.

On New Year's Day, 1962, he took a plane to Genoa, where he boarded the *Astoria* for Beirut. He had barely settled down in the ship's lounge before he met someone whose name he had ticked in the passenger-list. This was a man who was to ease his progress to an unexpected degree – Sheikh Majd el-Ard.

10

THE ROAD TO DAMASCUS

There was a fresh breeze blowing as the *Astoria* sailed from Genoa on the evening of January 1, 1962, and the passengers did not linger on deck. Cohen, travelling first class under the name of Kamal Amin Taabes, had an upper-deck cabin in the liner, near the officers' quarters. He took a last look at the old red buildings round the port, and retired to his cabin, where he unpacked his leather suitcase and the travelling bag that contained his precious "spy's own radio" disguised as an electric mixer. Then he made for the first-class bar so that he could have an aperitif and get to know some of his fellow-passengers.

With Salinger's help, he had ticked off some of the names on the passenger-list given him at Munich, and struck out others, so as to avoid wasting time on those who were going to places irrelevant to his purpose or were personally or socially of no account. What he wanted was people who, at the critical moment, might help him over certain obstacles on his journey to Damascus.

On board the *Astoria* he was once more absorbed into an Arab environment. Most of the ship's passengers came from the Middle East. The first-class included Egyptians, plenty of Lebanese, and a small number of Syrians. There were very few Europeans. January, with its rain, is not a good season for organised tours, and businessmen from Paris or Zurich tend to go by air to Cairo or Beirut.

All around him people were shouting and hurling questions at the tops of their voices, as Arabs do. Everyone was talking to everyone else at the same time. Despite variations of accent and some differences of phrasing, Arabs from Lebanon, Syria and Egypt understand one another perfectly without an interpreter.

Passengers on a short voyage, wherever they come from, form a temporary community, and behave quite differently from the way they react as individuals on dry land. The result here was to augment the unrestrained hubbub, and Cohen-Taabes was soon chatting away in the bar with one of the passengers whose name he had marked on the list. An hour later they were sharing a table in the first-class dining saloon: the agent had spotted his quarry, who had dashed right into the net.

The Sheikh Majd el-Ard was a slender figure, of average height, with markedly Semitic features and a sunburnt complexion; he wore good European clothes. Over their drinks in the bar they had exchanged the usual polite remarks and introduced themselves: Kamal Amin Taabes, a businessman of Syrian ancestry who lived in Argentina, was on his way to visit his parents' native land. His companion was an Arab of good position belonging to the ancient caste of feudal land-owners.

The Sheikh, indeed, owned an estate near Damascus. The social and Socialist revolutions that had shaken up the traditional feudalism of Syria's "good old days" had nonetheless left him master of "fellahin" – peasants who worked his land for a very poor percentage of the income it brought in.

Majd el-Ard also had business interests, and was re-turning in the *Astoria* from several months' travel in Europe which had taken him to Paris and Rome. He remarked to Kamal Taabes, with a smile: "Going to Europe is time well spent; there are plenty of charming places where one can have a pleasant time."

Elie Cohen realised at once how he could profit from the Sheikh's return to Damascus. He himself was not given to gossip, and even less inclined to exchange accounts of masculine exploits in shady Paris or Rome nightclubs. He gave the conversation a more serious turn and told the Sheikh how he had left Argentina, impelled by an earnest desire to come "home" and take an active part in the changing economic and political life of Syria.

The Sheikh was impressed by the young man's patriotic zeal, and over the dining table he discussed the situation in Syria from a viewpoint very different from that of Taabes' Baathist friends in Argentina. Leaning over towards Taabes so as not to be overheard, he said confidentially:

"Egyptian Socialism is dead, Allah be praised! We are free of that gang at last. The Egyptians have robbed us and taken everything. They came near confiscating our land to divide it amongst the peasants. Now, at least, we shall be able to breathe freely in Damascus."

He asked Taabes what he could do for him to make his home-coming easier. This was just the question Taabes had been waiting for since they met at the bar. As things stood, all he needed, beyond the introductions from his friends in Buenos Aires, was the company of a man like the Sheikh when he came to cross the Syrian frontier.

"I know no one, absolutely no one, in Damascus," he said. The Sheikh smiled and replied with the traditional Arab offer of hospitality: "My house is your house." He added: "I've just bought a new car in Europe, a Peugeot 404, which I've got on the boat. My young friend, you can rely on my friendship. When we get to Beirut consider yourself my guest.

And don't worry about being new in Damascus. You will find that my friends are yours."

They went on talking for hours. When Cohen-Taabes finally managed to slip back to his cabin, he felt he could claim that his first day on board the *Astoria* had been well spent: a rich Sheikh from Damascus was going to drive him there in a Peugeot 404 from Beirut, and would drop him right into the lion's den.

The crossing was uneventful. Salinger had advised Cohen, before he left Munich, to go ashore when the *Astoria* anchored at Alexandria and have his passport stamped. This would help to reassure the Syrian frontier officials when the time came. The spy put on a wide-brimmed hat and dark glasses, which would mask his face without provoking the curiosity of the Sheikh or other passengers, as a more elaborate disguise would have done. He had his passport examined and stamped, and then took a walk through the narrow streets of the port and the city, where so much of his youth had been spent.

Barely five years had passed since he had left Alexandria, and he knew every street. He could have gone into the shops and addressed their owners by name. He could have gone back to his own district and seen the house in which he had grown up. However, he resisted the temptation: in this city that seemed so unchanged he had no right to risk being recognised.

A ragged Arab child followed him with cries of "Baksheesh, Ya Sidi," holding out his hand. Elie Cohen, now Kamal Taabes, a tourist from Argentina, gave him a piastre. One thing he noticed was a decided increase in the number of soldiers and army lorries in the streets. He went back on board the *Astoria*, which resumed its voyage to Beirut, but he lingered on the upper deck, leaning on the railing until the last houses of Alexandria vanished on the horizon.

Beirut, where he landed next day, with his Syrian protector, Majd el-Ard, seemed, in contrast with Alexandria, to be
bursting with health and vitality. The capital of the "Switzerland of the Middle East", as Lebanon has been called, welcomed
passengers of the *Astoria* with a chorus of shouts and calls from
hawkers and porters josting along the quay. This Lebanese port
gave one the feeling of entering a world quite different from
Egypt, though no less Arab. Cohen had ample time to mark
the contrast, and to feel the noticeable throb of Beirut, a city
that seems to be perpetually seething with life.

He stood beside the Sheikh waiting for the dockers to
unload the new Peugeot from the hold. The Sheikh's various
suitcases and parcels, large and small, were piled higgledly-
piggledy in the car, with Kamal Taabes's more modest luggage.
Majd el-Ard kept on muttering "Let's hope the Syrian customs
don't give me any trouble – and that we get it over quickly . . ."
Cohen-Taabes could only echo in silence his protector's caution-
ary hopes. Whereas the Sheikh was simply worried about the
customs inspectors and the import duty he might have to pay
on the new car, Cohen-Taabes had more serious reasons for
being anxious about crossing the Syrian frontier.

But that frontier was still distant. "What about staying
on for 48 hours in this delicious city?" It was Majd el-Ard's
suggestion; Cohen, impatient as he was to get on to Damascus,
could only assent. They booked rooms at the Pla'ga (Beach)
Hotel and did the "Grand Dukes' Tour" of the city, making a
round of fashionable night-clubs, which satisfied them that there
was not much to choose between Beirut and Paris or Rome, as
far as night life is concerned.

Cohen-Taabes had good reason for satisfaction and for
showing the Sheikh that he was pleased and grateful. His first
steps on Arab soil were really like a pleasure trip. "Come to
Lebanon and enjoy its sunshine, its beauty, its zest for life:"
the official tourist posters turned out to be true, even for the

Israeli spy, Elie Cohen. He made up his mind to come back – and he did.

Sheikh Majd el-Ard and Kamal Taabes drove slowly towards the Syrian frontier. The narrow mountain road reminded the spy of the route from Naharya to Galilee, a few score miles to the south, on the other side of the Israeli frontier. He looked intently around, testing his memory, registering and mentally filing away his impressions of the journey.

At the Shtura Pass, the last Lebanese frontier post before reaching the Syrian control, there was a quick superficial baggage inspection and a purely formal scrutiny of passports. Noisy hawkers were offering to sell fruits and sweetmeats to motorists who were waiting for the barrier to be raised.

"Buy here; it's cheaper than Damascus. Make the most of it!" cried the hawkers. Kamal Taabes unhesitatingly reacted like a patriot: "We don't want anything. Keep your rubbish for the miserable people of Beirut." The Sheikh was delighted and clapped him on the shoulder, congratulating him on his patriotic spirit.

The barrier went up, and the Peugeot crossed the narrow no-man's land between the two frontiers. Here the road passes through a mountainous stretch, rocky, parched and treeless for hundreds of yards all round. As they got closer to the Syrian frontier, Cohen-Taabes observed the unmistakable signs of military fortifications; there had been none on the Lebanese side of the border. This first evidence of tension was in marked contrast to the complete peace of Lebanon. The evidence accumulated as the Sheikh's Peugeot drove deeper into Syria.

On the right, a notice informed travellers that they were now 1,910 metres (6,208 feet) above sea-level. A little further on was a second notice proclaiming in Arabic and Russian:

"For Moscow fly by Aeroflot" with the time-table of the twice-weekly service from Damascus to Moscow.

The Peugeot stopped before a six-foot-high barrier stretching right across the road, a real iron curtain. Syrian gendarmes appeared on either side of the car, accompanied by three soldiers armed with automatic machine-guns. Cohen-Taabes smiled, but his smile betrayed a certain tension, "Our Syrian brothers, at last!" he said. The Sheikh was equally ill at ease: if the customs officers showed themselves ill-disposed he would have to pay in duty as much as his new car had cost him. "I'm going to try to wangle things", he said, as he got out. "Stay in the car and wait for me".

Taabes did not move. He watched the Sheikh going to the customs-house, and silently contemplated a huge roadside notice just beyond the customs that displayed a map of the world showing Syria, all in red, at its centre. It was the first indication of the chauvinism he must henceforth expect at every step he took in Syria.

Something was happening at the customs. The Sheikh, in the distance, raised his arm and waved. Taabes did not catch on. He stayed where he was. The Sheikh ran over to the car, excited and beaming, followed by a Syrian in plain clothes. "I've met a friend – a very good friend who is in charge of the customs here. Come on out. Here he is."

Elie Cohen stepped out and set foot on the soil of Syria. It was a strange feeling, but the situation was comic and highly oriental.

"This is my friend Kamal Amin Taabes, a splendid chap. He has let a wonderful shipping business in Argentina go hang in order to come back to his home country," cried the Sheikh. Effusively, he flung an arm round Taabes's shoulder and introduced him to his friend from the customs. Then he raised his voice a little, to make sure of being heard: "This is my brother Nasser el-Din Waladi of the Syrian Security Service, who is in charge of this frontier post – Abu el-Din to his friends, and to you."

"My first meeting with Syria's Security Service": that was the thought that flashed through Cohen's mind. Before he had time to reflect that this meeting could on the whole be considered rather agreeable, he was holding out his hand to Abu el-Din, who shook it, exclaiming: "Welcome to your country."

Since the official in charge was looking after the travellers, no ordinary customs man came near the car. However other motorists arrived at the frontier post. Someone hooted, but no one moved; people don't hurry in the East. Still, Nasser Waladi signalled to the customs men to open the boot of the Peugeot and be quick about it. Taabes didn't even turn round. His luggage, (containing the mixer in which his miniature transmitter was hidden) lay in the boot, but it was at the bottom, under the Sheikh's suitcases.

The inspection was over; the customs men had done their duty and closed up the boot. The road lay open, and the official in charge of the frontier post – Abu el-Din to his friends – embraced both the sheikh and his protégé, Kamal Taabes, wishing them good luck in Damascus.

They got into the car again. The "iron curtain" opened in front of them: Syria was opening its doors to Elie Cohen, the Spy from Israel.

The Sheikh, in excellent humour, remarked to him. "That cost me 150 Syrian pounds (£15). A good chap, Abu el-Din; he didn't ask all that much. I imagine he must be very badly paid by the Security people."

The remarkable ease with which Cohen had crossed into Syria – thanks to his acquaintance on board ship with Sheikh Majd el-Ard – filled him with optimism for the future. There were moments when he really had the feeling that he was going "home", that he was the genuine Kamal Taabes, returning to the land of his parents.

The car wound its way slowly down the mountain slopes between the frontier and Damascus. The Sheikh pressed Taabes more than once to come and spend a few nights with him on his estate near the capital. Taabes politely refused, saying that he wanted to stay in Damascus and would take a room in a hotel.

"Then at least stay at a hotel kept by one of my friends," the Sheikh suggested. Taabes agreed with alacrity. So they stopped in front of one of the better-known hotels, the Semiramis. "You'll be perfectly all right here," said the Sheikh, and he asked the owner of the hotel, when he came out for Taabes's luggage, to "look after my friend just as you would look after me."

The date was January 10, 1962 – Elie Cohen's first day in Damascus.

11

"EIGHTY-EIGHT"

The Semiramis Hotel was not impressive. It had not changed in the least since it was built – early in the century. Whitewash and patches of blue were peeling off in flakes. The "best room" that the owner had been so proud to offer Taabes, on the recommendation of the Sheikh, was certainly large, but the furniture was rickety and the adjoining bathroom was not too clean.

Kamal Amin Taabes handed his Argentinian passport to the reception clerk, and while the police registration form was being filled in he amused himself by studying two official notices hanging up behind the reception desk. One of them, headed "Regulations of the Ministry of National Economy, paragraph 25", required hotel-keepers to "show consideration and courtesy to temporary visitors" and instructed the Syrian police to provide tourists with protection "free of charge and without recompense". The other notice listed the hotel prices, and stated that children under 16 were entitled to 50 per cent reduction and visitors' servants 30 per cent.

When he got to his room, Cohen-Taabes opened one of his suitcases and just unpacked the bare necessities. He had already decided to start looking for a flat right away. Although he was tired after the car journey, he was so excited to be in Damascus that he could not sleep for hours.

Next morning, the first thing he did was to telephone Sheikh el-Ard, as arranged explaining, somewhat untruthfully, that he was most comfortable in the hotel that his friend had recommended, but would nevertheless like to rent a flat of his own as soon as possible. The Sheikh promised to call for him in the afternoon. Meanwhile Cohen-Taabes took his first walk round the streets of Damascus.

A foreign tourist there, even if he comes from a neighbouring Arab country, is soon noticed by the passers-by – A European even sooner. Political instability, a succession of revolutions and *coups d'état*, and propaganda dinning it into the masses that "the enemy is listening at every door" – to quote the notices posted up in every public place – have resulted in the people of Damascus taking a very sharp interest in strangers.

Western visitors, such as French, American or other journalists who have spent a few days in the Syrian capital during recent years, invariably remark on this special sensitivity towards foreigners that makes Damascus unique among Arab capitals in the Middle East. Nowhere else does the experienced Western reporter find such difficulty in getting the man in the street to talk. Unkind observers go so far as to speak of a spy-fever raging in Damascus; the average Syrian has for the last ten or fifteen years been literally afraid of foreigners and, so far as possible, has shunned meeting them.

Syria, unlike other Arab countries such as Egypt, makes comparatively little call on foreign technicians and specialists for the purpose of economic and industrial development. The streets of Cairo and Alexandria are packed with foreigners. Some of them have special business to attend to; others are tourists from various countries – Western, African or Soviet. In Damascus it is far rarer to come across people who speak anything but Arabic, or who can be instantly labelled as foreigners. While one certainly finds in Syria an intellectual and technical ability well above the average level in other Arab countries, there has always existed there (and still does) a chauvinism fanatically insistent that the key positions in the administration and the economy shall be held by Syrian citizens.

One of the factors that brought the Union with Egypt to an end was the dismissal of Syrians from these same key-posts; their jobs were given to nominees from Cairo. In 1962 the only foreign specialists in Syria – and the same applies today – were members of Soviet military missions, experts in the use of the war material that poured into Syria, as it still does, from the U.S.S.R. These experts conduct themselves very discreetly in Syria, to avoid arousing the resentment of a touchy and self-assertive people.

Needless to say, this state of affairs did not make the Israeli spy's job easier. He had, however, one incomparable asset which no other foreigner possessed: his looks and his behaviour were completely adapted to the part he was to play, that of a long-lost son returning to his own country. Furthermore he had arrived in Damascus at a propitious time. The Union with Egypt had just come to an end. There was still complete confusion at the top, with tension between those whose only purpose was an independent Syrian nation and others still plotting to patch up the agreement with President Nasser's Government.

Both factions were looking for popular support and campaign funds. Kamal Taabes, a businessman who was supposed to have made a fortune in Argentina, was in a position to impress people with his numerous connections in Europe and South America. He could therefore win for the newly-installed régime in Damascus the support of the Syrian expatriates. This was, one might say, the key to the astounding success of the Israeli spy in Syria; for three years he was able to exploit the situation again and again.

In his special position as a Syrian whose home was in Argentina he led people to assume that he could rally overseas sympathisers with the régime, organise appeals for funds, and encourage other Syrian emigrants to invest capital in the country. This line of conduct had been laid down, in principle, during his last stay in Tel Aviv. As soon as he got to Damascus he pertinaciously and coolly adapted himself to it with a sort of infectious self-confidence. Certainly he played his part with such conviction that everyone who subsequently came into contact with him was forced to believe in it as much as he did.

He had asked Sheikh el-Ard over the telephone to give him a hand in finding a suitable flat, but when his good friend, happy to help his young compatriot, turned up at the hotel to keep his appointment, Taabes, in a state of obvious excitement, said he had changed his mind:

"There's something more urgent than the flat," he told the astonished Sheikh, who could hardly believe his ears. "I've made up my mind to settle in Damascus for good: I like this city, and I feel really at home here. I don't want to stay here just as a tourist with a visa like any foreigner's. What I want is a permanent residence permit. Couldn't you come with me here and now to the Ministry of the Interior, so that I can apply for one?"

The Sheikh was delighted to escort him to the Ministry, where he made his request. He simply had to fill in a form, and the Sheikh took the opportunity of telling the official in charge how highly he thought of Taabes and how much he hoped that there would be no delay in granting the permit.

During the next few days Taabes, usually accompanied by the Sheikh, called on a number of estate agents and flat-owners. He knew exactly what he was looking for: the ideal was a flat as close as possible to the General Staff Headquarters of the Syrian Army. He had studied plans of the city very carefully during his training at Tel Aviv, and knew that it was right in the centre of Damascus. It required some imagination on his part to find fresh reasons for rejecting offer after offer of flats in districts remote from Headquarters: the flats were found to be too large or too small or too expensive.

During his flat-hunting he learned to find his way about in Damascus. While the Sheikh was driving him round in the Peugeot 404, Taabes plied him with endless questions and displayed unconcealed curiosity about this or that building, monument or public park. The city bore no resemblance to Beirut, where he and his guide had spent two pleasant days. One missed the American cars and the liveliness of a city happily given over to pleasure and the joys of life. Damascus, where everyone wore Arab dress or badly-cut grey European suits, was more like an oriental version of a city behind the Iron Curtain. The cafés, overflowing at all hours of the day, made one think of beehives. The Syrian coffee-house, it has been said, is a substitute for a national sport, rather like the Paris bistro.

For Cohen-Taabes, these coffee-houses were to play an important part in his assignment. As soon as the Shiekh had introduced him to friends, whom he ran across in these noisy places, he realised that these were the focal points of public opinion in Damascus. One could take the pulse of the city in the cafés more reliably than anywhere else. In between cigarettes and tiny cups of hot, aromatic coffee a new Cabinet might be put together, Ministers might lose their heads or win office; in 1962 the popularity of the Baath party was soaring in the coffee-houses.

It might only be gossip and rumours that flew from table to table – dubious political tittle-tattle or unfounded assertions. All the same, the Spy learned to listen to the gossip of these Damascus coffee-houses. The chatter always contained a tiny fraction of truth, and it was this fraction that interested him.

Martyrs' Square, Damascus, where the captured Israeli armour was displayed after the Nukeib raid. This is where Elie Cohen was hanged.

General Abdel Karim Zahreddin, Syrian Commander-in-Chief
and uncle of Maazi Zahreddin.

In any case, he took no part in the conversation of the Sheikh and his friends. He listened, bearing in mind the Dervish's advice at Tel Aviv: "Don't be in any hurry. Keep your eyes open and listen. Slow, but sure, is the way to get on; you've plenty of time."

He had every reason to be pleased with his start in Damascus. Within 48 hours of his arrival he was strolling freely round the streets, sitting down at table in excellent company in the over-crowded coffee-houses, and still miles from arousing anyone's suspicions. The Syrian Security Service was certainly the last to imagine that a master-spy from Israel had just settled within its citadel.

Sheikh el-Ard also took him for a walk to another favourite resort of the people of Damascus – along the banks of the river Barada. Hundreds of families go picnicking on the verge of the river which has flowed through centuries of Middle Eastern history. Taabes and the Sheikh sat down on the grass, not far from a group of a dozen Syrian soldiers who were lying there and resting.

"Doesn't it strike you what a lot of soldiers one sees?" asked the Sheikh in all innocence. Without waiting for a reply, he lowered his voice and went on: "You know, there are even more secret agents all over our country than soldiers. Never speak your mind to anyone without knowing whom you're dealing with. They're simply everywhere!"

Cohen, who had no intention of unburdening himself to a stranger, was indeed to discover later that every Syrian party – Baath or anti-Baath, pro-Nasser or anti-Nasser – controlled a horde of agents. To be exact, they were not what are commonly called secret agents, but rather informers, either ordinary members or supporters of a given party, who would shuttle between their respective party offices and the coffee-houses, peddling political titbits and keeping their ears open among the little wooden tables where Shesh Besh was being played and coffee sipped. The Damascus coffee-houses are so closely linked with

H

different political groups, according to the affiliations of their customers, that the Syrian Secret Service, when they interrogate suspects, invariably ask them which coffee-houses they patronise.

After ten days in Damascus Taabes had still not found the flat he wanted. So he decided to approach a second contact. This was a man to whom he had obtained an introduction while in Argentina – Kamal Alheshan, the son of the editor of the Buenos Aires Arab weekly. Their meeting was to prove of major importance.

He rang him up on the strength of the letter from the elder Alheshan. Kamal was already in the picture, having had the promised letter from his father the previous summer, telling him that the "patriotic young man" would be coming to Damascus. They arranged to meet in a coffee-house the same day, and Kamal Taabes explained his housing problem to Alheshan, who expressed his willingness to help. Realising that the young Syrian trusted him from the start, Taabes put the situation to him:

"I'm looking for a place to live – somewhere I can use at the same time as an office for my import-export business. I'm going to settle in Damascus for good, so I need something permanent in a good neighbourhood, the Abu-Rumana district for instance".

He did not, of course, mention that the Syrian military Headquarters was located in this exclusive neighbourhood, and there was nothing to strike Alheshan as peculiar in the choice, since many business agencies, banks and head offices of industrial firms occupied buildings in Abu-Rumana. Several embassies, including that of India, were also situated there. So Kamal Alheshan promised to do his best to find him what he was looking for.

Two days later they met again and spent the afternoon

inspecting flats at Abu-Rumana, as well as several houses. However, Taabes had two reasons for being interested only in a flat in a large block. First, if he occupied a house by himself, he would have risked attracting the neighbours' attention to his (future) activities. Secondly, there was the problem of the antenna for his transmitter: he had to find a block with a number of television aerials on its roof, so that the one he proposed to erect would pass unnoticed.

Thanks to Kamal Alheshan, the spy finally discovered during the afternoon just what he had been looking for – a five-room flat in the Abu-Rumana district, reasonably well furnished in oriental, middle-class style. There were fine carpets in the sitting-room and bedroom. It was a comfortable flat, with a modern kitchen and good bathroom. With Alheshan's friendly help, he bargained with the owner and got the rent down to 3,900 Syrian pounds (380) a year. Finally, he moved in, transporting his suitcases in Alheshan's car.

Once there, Cohen wasted no time. He unpacked his luggage, took out his household equipment, including the mixer, dismantled it and exposed his miniature transmitter, the wonder-gadget that was to be his constant link with Israel. The electric light that hung from the ceiling of the bedroom had an enormous shade in the style of the early 1900s. Standing on a chair, he reached up and took down the lamp and the shade, and finally unscrewed the brass fitment – a sort of engraved saucer fixed to the ceiling – that covered the hole where the wiring came through. He satisfied himself that this would be the ideal hiding place for the transmitter.

To pick up messages from Israel all he needed was an ordinary radio receiver. There was none in the flat, so he had to buy one – a small standard Phillips model. Then he fixed up his antenna on the roof – it was the special flex from the electric razor with which he had been equipped at Tel Aviv. The neighbours were presumably used to seeing tenants putting up radio or television aerials on the roof. Anyhow, Cohen climbed up there in broad daylight, and went through the business of erecting the aerial which, seen from outside the house, looked like all the rest, though he was at pains to direct it fairly accurately in the direction of Israel.

It enabled him both to pick up and to transmit radio messages. All he needed was a small device to connect the radio receiver to the miniature transmitter. The flat was on the fourth floor, the top storey of the block, so the flex of the aerial ran up the outside wall to the roof – only a short distance. This short distance between the transmitter and the antenna reduced interference.

He had thought of a further advantage in living on the fourth floor. He later told his superiors in Israel that if he were caught he could jump from the fourth floor . . . and that would be the end.

When Cohen had finished setting up his radio equipment, he was free to gaze calmly out of the large centre window of his sitting-room: right opposite his flat stood the Headquarters of the Syrian Army, its roof bristling with aerials. Barbed wire fences all round it kept the public at a distance. Heavily armed sentries guarded each corner.

At nine o'clock in the evening on February 12, 1962, Elie Cohen put the transmitter to use for the first time, sending a short series of prearranged signals to Israel. He was calling the Intelligence Staff at Tel Aviv, and was quickly picked up. Within a few seconds, he was delighted to get the answer back from Israel: "Standing by to receive you."

He tapped out the identity number arranged with Tel Aviv – "Eighty-eight", which also meant "Found flat, am starting work". But neither he nor Tel Aviv had foreseen that he would then add two words in code, i.e. "Opposite Headquarters". He thought it well to make it clear where the flat was and what sort of people lived across the way.

The Dervish read his message that night, and drew a thick red line under the words "Opposite Headquarters". His pupil seemed to be making out pretty well in Damascus.

12

NUKEIB

The initiative for any action was left for the moment with Elie Cohen. His superiors at Tel Aviv were not going to ask him any questions or give him any specific task before they knew exactly what his capabilities were; this they could judge only by the level of information that he was able to feed them.

He began, very reasonably, by examining his immediate neighbourhood, i.e. the Syrian General Staff Headquarters facing his window. He systematically watched the comings and goings in and out of the building, so as to be able to spot anything peculiar or unusual. For the first few days he kept watch from eight in the morning, when the Headquarters started to come to life, till six in the evening, when most of the officers and clerks left the building.

He noticed, after keeping watch for several evenings, that only five rooms remained lit up all night, and deduced that they were occupied by night duty officers. It could be assumed that these belonged to the Military Intelligence Operations Branch. The general outlook in Damascus during the first half of February was calm, and Elie took it that the almost complete darkness – apart from the five rooms – in the Staff Headquarters was the normal routine.

Under his alias of Kamal Amin Taabes, Elie frequently met young Kamal Alheshan, and was introduced by him to several of his friends. He asked all of them, especially those in official positions, about the difficulties in exporting Syrian goods to Europe. He told them that he had a fair sum deposited abroad in Swiss and Belgian banks. With this capital and his European connections, Taabes proposed to export to Europe Syrian furniture and *objets d'art*, always assuming that Syrian officialdom did not prove too obstructive.

Gradually his circle of acquaintances grew. Young Taabes, introduced everywhere by his friend Alheshan (who had an excellent reputation among business people in Damascus), made himself universally popular. People trusted him almost at sight, and his scheme for exporting Syrian furniture and *objets d'art* met with general approval and encouragement.

He was asked one day by Kamal Alheshan why he did not buy a car: "It would make your business visits easier; you waste a lot of valuable time walking from place to place." His reply was that he'd had enough of the Cadillac life in Buenos Aires, and now preferred to walk, like the common man.

On his front door he had put up a small visiting card inscribed "Import-Export, Taabes". His modest behaviour and unobtrusive patriotism helped him gain the sympathy and friendship of many who met him in Damascus.

His first opportunity to do Israeli Intelligence an important service occurred much sooner than he had expected. As soon as he had signalled "88", to convey the fact that he had settled down in Damascus, he ought in theory to have broken off all radio contact with Tel Aviv for weeks or even months, so as to dig himself in. "Don't rush things", it had been dinned into him. However, events took an unforeseen turn.

At seven in the evening on March 8, 1962 he heard an

announcement over Radio Damascus: "Today our gallant soldiers have inflicted a crushing defeat on the troops of our Zionist enemy. The Syrian Army has damaged Zionist warships on the Sea of Galilee. The enemy suffered severe losses, and withdrew before the Syrian Army."

In the absence of any definite knowledge, he could guess that this announcement was a long way from the truth. The Syrians had again fired on Israeli fishing boats on the Sea of Galilee, which the United Nations recognised as coming under Israel's sovereignty. They had also opened fire on an Israeli patrol boat which had come to the aid of the fishermen. Two men in the patrol boat had been wounded by Syrian shots.

This serious incident was discussed at the weekly meeting of the Israeli Cabinet, which decided to take measures to prevent a recurrence. Meanwhile, the radio announcement had put Cohen on the alert, and he resumed his watch on the Syrian General Staff, concealing himself behind the curtains of the window that overlooked the Headquarters. He noticed at once that there was unusual activity round and inside the building. Nearly all the windows that had previously been dark were lit up all night.

Next day he saw Alheshan and, for the first time, tried to turn the conversation to the political and military situation in Syria, but he did not get very far. Alheshan did not show much inclination to discuss the subject with him, and Taabes, discreet and cautious as usual, did not pursue it. In the evening he took up his watch again by the window, but this time everything was quiet and normal: lights shone only from the usual five windows.

A further Cabinet meeting was summoned by Ben-Gurion in Jerusalem on March 11, and the position on the Syrian frontier was the only topic discussed. What the Israeli Government wanted to know was whether the incidents on the Sea of Galilee were the direct result of the permanent state of tension in this area or whether, on the other hand, they reflected a deliberate decision on the part of the Damascus Government to prove to Nasser that, despite its rift with Egypt, Syria was still the most strongly anti-Israeli element in the Arab world.

The Israeli Cabinet considered the situation sufficiently serious to grant full powers to the ministerial Defence Committee under Ben-Gurion himself. The next day, this special committee decided to retaliate in force if the Syrians again resorted to hostile action.

Cohen, alone in Damascus, was cut off from all sources of Israeli information, and knew nothing of the decisions taken in Jerusalem. However, he suddenly noticed that the number of military vehicles in the streets of Damascus, especially tank-transporters, had increased since the day of the incident on the Sea of Galilee.

There was no one he could question, since as yet he had no reliable source to go to for that sort of information. He reflected that all this military activity in the streets of Damascus might perhaps herald an Army coup. But he had another reason for assuming that the tension on the Israeli frontier was the cause of all the military commotion in the capital. For the first time since Cohen had arrived in Damascus, the Syrian press was devoting editorials to the "Zionist danger" and preparing public opinion for a renewal of hostilities. While drinking a cup of coffee in the Hamdia Market, the traditional oriental bazaar in the Old City, he got a definite impression of unusual excitement, indicating something in the wind.

He had still not had any order or specific directive from Tel Aviv, but only the signal, the day he had moved into his flat, acknowledging receipt of his message; since then, total silence. However, he felt intuitively that the moment had probably come to communicate with Israel, where they might be in need of his assistance.

He was surprised that night to find all the windows of

the General Staff Headquarters lit up again, but he waited another day, and when, at nightfall, he noticed an unusual amount of activity at Headquarters, he decided to send Tel Aviv his first operational message. Double-locking his front door, he drew the curtains, removed his miniature transmitter from its hiding place above the ceiling lamp, drafted his text in Hebrew, and then, seated on his bed, called Tel Aviv.

It was about 8.30 in the evening, and the date was March 13, 1962. Within minutes he got back the agreed signal that he was being satisfactorily received. With the Hebrew text balanced on his knee, he ciphered it from memory and tapped it out. This first brief message ran as follows:

"Staff headquarters busy, lit up three nights running. Abnormal troop movements in city streets. Believe Syrian army in state of alert. Military coup unlikely. Virulent anti-Israel attitude in local press. Consider alert directed against Israel."

His message was received, and Tel Aviv simply acknowledged by the agreed signal, which Cohen picked up on his Phillips radio set. Nothing more was heard: Elie Cohen was alone again. He dismantled his transmitter, tucked it into its hiding place, and tuned in his radio to the local station. He lit a match, burnt the paper on which he had written the message, and swilled the ashes down the sink.

He had not been mistaken. On March 14 the Israeli Army Staff had a message from forward positions on the Syrian frontier: "Tanks and armour have just been positioned at fortified Syrian posts on the hills around Sea of Galilee. Uninterrupted troop movements from rear towards frontier."

Cohen's message did not merely corroborate the reports from Israeli forward positions: it made it plain that the troop movements were not made on the initiative of a local commander, but resulted from a central directive of the Syrian General Staff. That was how the Israeli General Staff interpreted the connection between the lit-up windows of the

Damascus Headquarters and the military lorries without head-
lights that were moving fresh troops towards the frontier. The
immediate Israeli reaction to these reports that Cohen had
confirmed was to reinforce her frontier positions round the Sea
of Galilee.

By Friday, March 16, the full scope of the Syrian plan
was clear. The Damascus Government had resolved to strike a
decisive blow against Israeli fishing in the Sea of Galilee, thereby
disputing the sovereignty of Israel over this part of its territory.
There had been a change of tactics, and the Syrians now wanted
open battle with Israel, even if it meant bringing the question
of Israeli sovereignty before United Nations arbitration.

Fighting broke out at ten in the morning, when Israeli
fishermen, escorted by a police patrol-boat, were preparing to
pull in their nets. The Syrian military posts at Nukeib, Kursi
and Masoudieh opened a steady fire on the Israeli fishing boats
and their escort. This was a more serious attack than the
previous one – sustained shelling by Soviet-made non-recoiling
guns.

The sound of the shelling reached Ben-Gurion, who was
staying at the lakeside Galei Kinneret hotel, facing the hills
where the Syrian guns were sited. Twenty minutes after the
firing had started the Chief of Staff, General Zvi Tsur, and the
Commander of the Northern Sector, Meir Zoreya, called on
him. The Prime Minister, to whom the Cabinet had entrusted
full powers, gave the order to move in on the attacking Syrian
positions and silence the guns.

During the course of that evening several Israeli regiments were concentrated at Kibbutz Ein-Gev. At about midnight they set out to attack the enemy position at Nukeib. The
Israeli General Staff knew that the Syrian Army was in a state
of alert and had consequently arranged for reinforcements to be
ready to move in from other parts of the area. The Air Force,
too, was ordered to be in a state of readiness.

The Battle of Nukeib, known as the "Battle of March 16", though really it went on till 4 a.m. next day, was unusually fierce and bloody. A little after midnight the first Israeli troops to push their way into Syria stumbled upon a minefield. The entire valley of the Jordan was lit up all that night by shelling.

Units from the Golani Infantry Division who eventually took the Nukeib position demolished it, down to the last earthwork. The Syrians countered by shelling Kibbutz Ein-Gev and destroying a good part of the houses, whose occupants had taken refuge in the air raid shelters. Finally the Israeli Air Force joined in and bombed all the Syrian frontier positions along the hills that encircle the Sea of Galilee.

Driven out of the bunkers and dug-outs of Nukeib, the Syrians left dozens of casualties behind them; the officer in command being among the dead. The Israelis took back some valuable battle-trophies – seven types of weapon and ammunition, all supplied by Russia, and one prisoner, the 21-year-old private Ji'hye Hassin.

The Israelis had once more shown bravery in battle, but they had one major handicap. On this sector of the frontier all the Syrian positions stand on the hills, and their artillery and machine-guns can range on targets at a lower level; the Israeli positions lie along a narrow strip of plain bordering the Sea of Galilee. This disadvantage was costly to the Israelis, who lost three armoured half-tracks on the minefield where their troops first entered enemy territory. Eight Israeli soldiers had lost their lives while storming the hill. A ninth soldier, called Yaakov Devir, was reported missing.

At a press conference held at Tel Aviv on the Saturday night, when the Chief of Staff gave a detailed account of the battle, he stated that nothing was known of the missing man. Some little time later Elie Cohen was instructed to find out what had become of him.

Meanwhile Cohen, in Damascus, was weighing up the serious situation engendered by the clash at Nukeib. The local radio told him that three Israeli armoured vehicles had been left in the minefield. Damascus admitted the loss of five men, but naturally talked of "the Syrian victory over the Zionist enemy."

Two days after the fighting, on the Monday night, Kamal Alheshan turned up without warning at Cohen's flat with a young Syrian lieutenant in uniform. This was the first time that Kamal Alheshan had called on him without warning, and Cohen was sufficiently startled to eye his callers with some anxiety, wondering what this visit could mean.

Alheshan, observing his surprise, excused himself. "I just took a chance. I wasn't sure I'd find you in." His voice sounded as friendly as ever, and Taabes showed his two guests into the sitting-room and offered them a drink.

"May I introduce a good friend of mine?" asked Alheshan. He seemed to be proud of this friendship. He went on: "Lieutenant Maazi Zahreddin." Then he paused and added: "His uncle, Abdel Karim Zahreddin, is Chief of Staff of the Syrian Army."

It was a name Cohen knew well. Abdel Karim Zahreddin was famous in Syria at the time, and just as well known in Israel, where his photograph often appeared in the papers. If this really was a courtesy call, as Alheshan claimed, the young lieutenant's arrival in Cohen's flat was heaven-sent. But he still needed to make sure that it was just that, and nothing more.

While he was in the kitchen, brewing his two guests Turkish coffee, Cohen thought things over, and his anxieties soon vanished. He overheard Alheshan and the lieutenant discussing political and military topics loudly and without any inhibition. Nor did they change the subject when he rejoined them in the sitting-room.

Maazi Zahreddin displayed some curiosity about the great world that Taabes (according to Alheshan) knew so well

– Europe and South America. The young lieutenant, with his future as a Syrian officer still before him, had never been out of his country, apart from one brief visit to Beirut.

Taabes, in his role of patriot, rebuked the young man: "All the wealth of Argentina is worth less than the happiness of living here in Syria, our own country." He spoke emphatically, in a tone that Alheshan knew well, but the young lieutenant was suitably impressed.

Still the ardent patriot, he added: "If my business responsibilities here were not so pressing, I think I should have volunteered for the Army. They must be needing men at the moment for the war against the Zionists."

The lieutenant made no comment, but Alheshan kept the ball rolling: "We've got a dangerous situation here in Damascus, too. The Army is getting very popular, and there are certain officers who might exploit the situation and overthrow the Government. This would cause fresh chaos in this country, just as we're struggling to recover from the last political upheaval."

Maazi nodded in agreement. "The Israelis won at Nukeib, for all the heroism of our men. I just wonder whether we're in a position to retaliate effectively. Their Air Force is first-class, whereas ours is still weak and, what's more, badly trained by Israeli standards. Not to mention the Migs the Egyptians have collared and refuse to give back. The planes that Moscow has promised us are a long time coming."

Cohen, pouring out the coffee, did not miss a word. His face did not betray his feelings. "Even our Syrian 'eagles' will not get far without planes," he remarked in a tone of gloom. He deliberately used the word "eagles", knowing that this was how Syrian patriots habitually referred to their airmen.

The Israeli spy could well suppose that the young lieutenant, who belonged, like his uncle, to Syria's Druse minority, was better informed of the state of the Army than many officers of higher rank. And Maazi, no doubt encouraged by Alheshan's calling Taabes "my brother Kamal", was only too eager to talk. However, Cohen, wary of rousing the young man's suspicions, took care, for the moment, not to ask any indiscreet questions, apart from one small query: "I suppose you must be pretty familiar with the Nukeib fighting area?"

The question did not surprise Maazi. "Do I know the area? Why, last Wednesday, two days before the fighting, I was on a tour of inspection of all the Syrian positions around the Sea of Galilee. I've seen the enemy defence works with my own eyes."

Cohen could not resist saying with a laugh: "You know, I always avoided Jews in Argentina, although there are plenty of them there. But Jewish soldiers carrying weapons – that I'd love to see, even from a distance."

The lieutenant explained that civilians were forbidden to enter the military zones along the frontiers. The very few who, for one reason or another, were allowed in had to carry a special pass, which was extremely difficult to get. "This place is crawling with Zionist spies," he added darkly, in the tone of one who has some inside knowledge.

Cohen did not pursue the matter, but Maazi, after a pause, went on. "One of these coming Fridays we'll all go and have a look at the military zone, the three of us. I'll take you in my car, then we won't have any bother at Army check-points."

Alheshan, not too keen on a trip to the front, said he'd already done the round about a year earlier, and Taabes teased him: "Are you afraid of Zionist bullets?" Alheshan denied this vehemently, and it was agreed to make an early tour of the front, when things were a little quieter. Meanwhile the Chief of Staff's nephew produced another piece of priceless information for the benefit of the Israeli spy.

The young man told him that Brigadier Abdel Karim Nahalawi was at odds with the Government. "Nahalawi (he said) is at the moment Syria's strong man. He thinks all our Ministers are incompetent. My uncle is trying to persuade him to give the present Government another chance, but Nahalawi won't hear of it. In view of the frontier situation after the battle of Nukeib, he's convinced that the people only believe in the Army. I'm sure that the Colonel won't hesitate to bring about changes in the Government in the very near future."

It was just on midnight when Alheshan and Maazi left. The young lieutenant, as he said goodbye, asked the spy to go to the cinema with him later in the week.

Elie Cohen, alone in his flat at last, took a look at the building opposite. It took him some hours to summarise in brief and precise terms everything he had just found out from Lieutenant Maazi Zahreddin. As before, he made a written draft before ciphering it and sending it off that same night.

The message contained two pieces of information that the Israeli Intelligence noted with interest:

(a) The Syrian Air Force was frightened of the Israeli Air Force; the Egyptians refused to hand over to Syria the Migs they had taken.

(b) While some Syrian army officers did not disguise their dissatisfaction with a Government that they considered too "soft", the strong man of the moment was still Brigadier Nahalawi.

On this occasion Cohen quoted the source of his information, and did so, as he said later, with some pleasure. Henceforward he proposed referring to Maazi Zahreddin in his messages simply as "M" – in cipher of course. The number corresponding to the letter "M" was to recur endlessly in messages he sent during his next three years in Syria.

That particular night he did not get to sleep until daybreak.

The Israeli General Staff at Tel Aviv was making urgent demands on the Intelligence Service for information about

Sami el-Jundi, Minister of Information, and Cohen's
boss when he worked for the Syrian Radio.

Syrian Prime Minister Salah el-din el-Bitar.

The dock during the trial (Elie Cohen is first on the left, front row).

Syrian intentions. The first part of Cohen's message was interpreted as foreshadowing reduced tension on the frontier. If it
were true that the Syrians were short of aircraft and afraid of
the strong potential of the Israeli Air Force, they would avoid
widening their sphere of operations.

At first light on March 19, and again on March 21,
Syrian Mig-17s flew along the frontier, but not one machine
ventured into Israeli air space.

The Israeli Cabinet held a special meeting in Jerusalem
on March 20, which went on into the night. The Chief of
Staff, and the then head of the Secret Service, Isser Harel, were
present, and joined Ben-Gurion and his Ministers in a political
and strategic survey. It was the general view that in essence the
risk of a wholesale conflict with Syria had temporarily receded.
The Cabinet resolved to pursue a political and diplomatic
course at the United Nations and in all the major capitals, to
counteract the Syrian campaign against Israel's sovereign rights
over the Sea of Galilee and the perpetually-disputed frontier
area.

Ben-Gurion also decided to reinforce the Israeli delega-
tion in New York with a special adviser, General Meir Amit,
the head of the Military Intelligence Service (Modi'in). This
highly respected officer had shown his ability in the past and was
better equipped than anyone to discuss the practical problems
of this frontier area.

It will be seen that Elie Cohen's speedy and perceptive
work in the heart of Syria produced immediate results, and
directly influenced the moderate and considered decisions that
the Jerusalem Cabinet then adopted.

There was a further sequel to the fighting at Nukeib that
the Israeli spy found disagreeable. Towards the end of March
the Syrian radio and newspapers persuaded the people of

Damascus "to see with their own eyes the booty won by our valiant troops in their battle against the Zionists". Official propaganda had transformed the Syrian defeat at Nukeib into a dazzling victory, and everything had been done to glorify the Army and increase its prestige. The three Israeli armoured vehicles abandoned in the minefield were brought to Damascus and put on view in the Martyrs' Square.

Crowds poured in to see the spoils captured from the Israelis. Elie Cohen had great difficulty in fighting his way through the mob that greeted the sight of enemy armour with shouts of "Death to the Zionists" or "Long live the heroes of Syria!"

The three half-tracks were grouped as a triangle in the middle of the Square, and the crowd paraded round them. If he had not seen this display of fanaticism for himself, Cohen would not have thought such scenes possible. Thousands of Syrians filed past and dozens of them stroked and even embraced the vehicles captured from Israeli troops; others just spat on them. There was no doubt whatever that they were all inspired by the same feelings of patriotic pride in their Army and hatred of Israel.

A few rather battered petrol tanks with Hebrew lettering on them had been placed alongside the half-tracks, to "prove" that the Syrians had shot down Israeli aircraft. But Cohen was able to see there and then that they were really containers from Syrian Air Force Mig 17s, not from the Israeli Vautours that had taken part in the Nukeib fighting.

In the midst of this crowd of over-excited Syrians, with the armoured vehicles captured from his own country's Army before his eyes, the Spy from Israel felt the full weight of his isolation. He could not foresee that three years later, almost to the day and the hour, the same crowd would come to the same place to gaze at another spectacle – Elie Cohen, the Spy from Israel, on the gallows.

The depressing scene that he had witnessed in Martyrs' Square affected Cohen deeply. He sensed more strongly than ever the latent danger of Arab fanaticism, which could incite this country to unbridled action against Israel. He felt compelled, more than ever before, to do his best to fulfil his dangerous assignment.

The next opportunity soon presented itself. He had hardly got back to his flat from Martyrs' Square before his telephone rang: "Kamal Taabes? Good. What about coming to the cinema this evening?" The voice was Maazi Zahreddin's. "Delighted," said Cohen-Taabes. So the same evening he was at the Dounia ("World") cinema, sitting next to the nephew of the Syrian Chief of Staff, watching a film about the epic attack on Rommel's headquarters in Libya by British commandos.

Around midnight they found a table in a café near the cinema. The young lieutenant was still very excited by the film; he had been very impressed by the professional handling of the attack. Out of the blue, he exclaimed: "Just imagine the Israelis playing the same trick on us!"

The spy restrained an impulse to laugh aloud, and asked: "What gives you that idea? Are the Israelis so strong? Or are we so weak?"

Zahreddin said: "My answer to each of your questions is Yes."

That night Cohen realised that he had taken a real liking to the young Syrian officer; and this had nothing to do with the invaluable help that he was going to get from him. Maazi Zahreddin looked you straight in the face with his brown eyes. His patriotism, barely tinged by hatred of Israel, was sincere and real. His readiness to fight for his country and his pride in being a Syrian were just the traits that would appeal to Elie Cohen. What the spy did not yet know, but would soon discover, was that the lieutenant's feelings for him were just as close.

13

THE MISSING CORPORAL

Nothing had been heard of the 19-year-old Israeli corporal, Yaakov Devir, reported missing after the battle of Nukeib, and inquiries were launched through the United Nations Armistice Commission. He might be dead or wounded or simply a prisoner. The reply came back from the Syrians a few days later: he was not in their hands, either living or dead.

Nonetheless, Israelis remained convinced that he was somewhere in Syria. From past experience it was known that the Syrians were capable of keeping Israeli citizens, who for one reason or another had crossed the frontier and fallen into their hands, in prison for years under conditions of secrecy. It was physically impossible for a shell to have obliterated the corporal without trace. Until there was proof that Devir was dead, his parents (who lived near Tel Aviv) and the Israeli Army Command were bound to believe that he was still alive in a prison or hospital somewhere in Syria. So after a time Elie Cohen was asked by the Intelligence Service to find out what he could.

Meanwhile, despite the continuing frontier tension, he was busy setting up his import–export business, so as to make his assumed personality the more convincing. During his first weeks in Damascus he had made contact with a number of manufacturers and businessmen with a view to interesting them in exporting to Europe – especially to Munich and Zurich – hand-made Damascus tables of the type used for playing Shesh-Besh; one finds them in most Syrian and Lebanese coffee-houses and restaurants. He also came upon *objets d'art* of various kinds made locally, antique and modern jewellery, and an assortment of leather-work. In his opinion all these goods could find a market in Europe.

The spy was careful to tell businessmen that he was in touch with a substantial import firm in Europe, whose main offices were in Munich and Zurich. Through these contacts he could export the *objets d'art* and the traditional tables, which he said were in much demand in Europe. His negotiations gave him the excuse to correspond with the firm's chief European agent – none other than his friend and "Resident Director", Salinger.

He sent Salinger a succession of genuine business letters setting forth the feasibility of buying *objets d'art* in Damascus, with particulars of price, conditions of sale and credit. From time to time he enclosed detailed catalogues that he had obtained from dealers in Damascus. Naturally Salinger's firm replied, thus setting in train a flow of correspondence between the spy and his "Resident Director" in Europe. Eventually this correspondence enabled Cohen to send the Israeli Secret Service, via Munich and Zurich, a variety of information and even microfilms. But before it had got very far another dramatic development changed the political scene in Syria.

In the small hours of March 28, Damascus Radio, which had been playing martial music for an hour, broadcast an announcement introduced as "Communiqué 26", implying that this was a proclamation by the Army. "Syrian Army Head-quarters", listeners were told, "has taken over the conduct of the nation's business, in order to ensure the country's political stability and guarantee the rights and civil liberties of its citizens. Any attempt to oppose measures taken by the General

Staff of the Army will be severely punished. The frontiers, ports and airports will remain closed till further notice." The proclamation was signed by Brigadier Nahalawi.

Cohen was already on the watch from behind the curtains of his sitting-room. He could see that the Staff Headquarters building was surrounded by a guard of Syrian tanks. Further communiqués signed by Colonel Nahalawi were broadcast, one of which declared that the previous Government had tried to sow discord in Army circles. Another proclaimed that "the Palestine problem will be in the forefront of the Army's deliberations. The Syrian Army will do everything in its power to free Palestine from its Zionist invaders."

Cohen had known from Maazi Zahreddin of Brigadier Nahalawi's intention to make changes in the Government, and had at once sent the news to Tel Aviv. He tried to get hold of the young officer that morning, but got no answer when he telephoned.

So Cohen decided to make a round of the coffee-houses, where he was sure to glean some early news and rumours about the coup and the top people behind it. He rang up Sheikh el-Ard and asked him to meet him at a coffee-house they both knew, but the Sheikh preferred to stay at home as long as the situation was still obscure. Kamal Alheshan, on the other hand, was as keen as Kamal Taabes to find out more about what was going on. It was two days before Cohen met Maazi Zahreddin with Alheshan and succeeded in getting first-hand information.

The very night after Nahalawi's coup Cohen had had a radio inquiry from Tel Aviv, putting a series of brief concrete questions to him about the coup itself and the leading figures involved. On the strength of what he had found out from his friends, he was able to give satisfactory answers, and from March 28 until practically the end of April he was sending messages regularly. Every night, usually between eight o'clock and ten o'clock but sometimes later, he would close the shutters and the front door, get his miniature transmitter out of its hiding-place, make contact with Tel Aviv, wait for the acknowledgment signal, and send his ciphered message over the air.

For a whole month he provided a constant stream of political information. His messages were picked up, deciphered at once, and forwarded the same night by the Secret Service to the Israeli General Staff. A digest of his information was usually on the Prime Minister's desk the next morning.

To Cohen's great delight, Maazi's uncle, Abdel Karim Zahreddin, remained Chief of the Syrian General Staff. He himself saw Maazi at least ten times between March 30 and the end of April and what the young man told him, including the latest Army gossip and scandals, provided the basis for the messages he sent to Tel Aviv. The gist of his information was that the officers who had overthrown the Government were the same men who, a few months earlier, had precipitated the collapse of the Union with Egypt.

The Chief of the General Staff, and the Army as such, had not taken part in the actual coup, but they had given their blessing to the action of Brigadier Nahalawi, the "strong man" who had pulled the wires. Nahalawi, a man of forty and a moderate conservative, was a senior officer in the Defence Ministry who had been Chief Military Assistant to the Egyptian Governor of Syria, Marshal Abdul Hakim Amer.

In the "Revolutionary Council" which temporarily acted as a Government, Nahalawi's second string was Brigadier Abdel Ghani Dahman, the Military Commander of Damascus. Between them the two men had set up a military régime to preserve Syria's national independence and to forestall renewed subjection to Cairo. At the same time, they were endeavouring to resume relations with Nasser on a basis of honourable and mutual respect. Military opinion, Cohen pointed out in his messages, expected no major change in the position on the Israeli frontier.

More than once it was found that information that he sent overnight was officially confirmed during the course of the next day. Thus on March 30 the Chief of Staff, Zahreddin, held a press conference in Damascus which was broadcast by the local radio. This was monitored in Tel Aviv, but it was not known there that their agent, Elie Cohen, was actually among the local and foreign correspondents present. He had been invited by the General's nephew, Maazi Zahreddin.

Cohen realised during the press conference that the officers who had overthrown the Government preferred to keep out of the limelight and leave the Chief of Staff the honour of taking the stage. Since Zahreddin belonged to the Druse minority,* he to some extent afforded a guarantee that the Army would not make any attempt to wrest power from the civil arm. As a professional soldier the General enjoyed an unassailable prestige among the ordinary people; on the other hand, it would be unthinkable for a Druse to aspire to the highest political position in a country with a Moslem majority.

After this press conference Cohen explained to Tel Aviv that General Zahreddin was no more than a screen behind which Nahalawi and his team of officers led by Brigadier Dahman were hidden. It was they alone who were in a position to take the decisions which mattered, irrespective of any impression that the General's speeches might give.

Another crucial political development occurred two days later, on April 2. That morning there was a local military rising in the town of Aleppo, in the north of Syria, where a small group calling itself "The Free Officers" declared itself in revolt against the Damascus Government. These officers preached a revival of the Union of Syria and Egypt, and among their demands was the purging from the Supreme Army Com-

* The Druse tribesmen, mostly to be found in Syria, Lebanon and Israel, form an esoteric sect that broke away from Islam in the 10th century, acknowledge a different prophet and hold a different creed.

mand of all officers responsible for the *coup d'état*. Just before
the declaration of the "Free Officers" in Aleppo there had been
serious disturbances in several cities, including Homs. A state
of siege was declared in both cities, and after clashes between
troops and police had led to casualties, some fatal, the country
seemed to be veering towards civil war.

The rebel officers in Aleppo telephoned the Egyptian
Embassy in Lebanon for reinforcements. The Israeli spy (who
was unlikely to attract any unfriendly scrutiny in these conditions of renewed chaos) received an urgent inquiry from Tel
Aviv, asking whether the revolutionary officers in Damascus
would retain power in face of the rebel "Free Officers". His
answer the same day ran as follows:

"Homs and Aleppo rebel officers' struggle against
Damascus authorities has speeded fall of revolutionary military
caste. Expect imminent fall of promoters of last coup."

Once more, the spy was right, thanks to first-class
information backed up by a correct assessment of the situation
and the respective powers of the two sides. On April 3, barely 36
hours after the rising in the North, Brigadiers Nahalawi and
Dahman and five of their companions in misfortune fled
secretly to Lebanon, where they caught a plane to Zurich. The
Swiss Government granted them tourist visas, and they settled
into a luxury hotel in Lausanne.

There was the usual unhappy sequel to a squabble
between the military leaders of the Syrian Republic: the
civilians behind the Army coup were left to bear the brunt.
Syria found herself politically leaderless overnight, and there
was a general state of upheaval. General Zahreddin alone
stayed where he was as Chief of Staff; his nephew Maazi told
Cohen-Taabes that the General had no intention of meddling in
politics, but the civilian leaders were reluctant to resume
authority.

The day after Nahalawi's flight Maazi called at Taabes's

flat. "My uncle hasn't slept for a week," he told his friend. "He's doing his best to encourage certain prominent men to head the Government, but I doubt if he'll manage it. Not one of them wants to risk his neck."

Taabes asked him who, in the circumstances, could take charge of Syria's fortunes. "I'll tell you in confidence," said Maazi; "for the moment, this must be kept completely secret." He went on to explain that the Chief of Staff had been in touch that very day with a veteran politician, Dr. Nazim el-Kudsi, and suggested that he should at once again become President of the Republic.*

Taabes, playing on the young lieutenant's ambitions without his realising it, asked him whether he was playing any personal part in all these political moves. "Not before I get to major," said Maazi.

On April 14 the Tel Aviv "Head Office" picked up the following message from Cohen:

"Three distinct groups of officers are at present at work on the Army:

"(a) the main group (which includes Nahalawi's supporters) fighting for national independence and opposed to any fresh merger with Egypt;

"(b) a group (chiefly of officers from the Division defending the frontier with Israel) that claims to consist of Socialists;

"(c) a small group of pro-Nasser officers without any real influence on the general situation."

From this the logical conclusion was drawn at Tel Aviv that as long as internal struggles continued in Syria relative calm could be expected along the frontier.

Piecing together the information from Cohen and other sources, people in Israel were able to deduce that the battle of Nukeib had had an indirect but decisive effect on the recent

---

* He had been elected President on December 16, 1961 and had remained in office until the coup of March 28.

political developments in Syria. Nahalawi had rightly judged it necessary to reinforce the Syrian positions along the frontier, for fear of a fresh Israeli attack there. But, in doing so, he had sawn off the branch on which he was perched. When the Homs and Aleppo risings took place, the help of trusty friends could have saved the ruling military clique from collapse; but the officers concerned were on the frontier, and therefore not available.

Finally, Tel Aviv concluded in April – and proof of this can be found in black and white in Elie Cohen's personal file – that their man in Damascus had managed to establish himself firmly in the city, and in record time. His "cover" among businessmen was impeccable; his circle of acquaintances was growing each week; he behaved at all times and under all circumstances like a genuine Syrian patriot. At the same time, his messages and information were completely accurate, and showed how unerringly he could analyse the situation and predict future developments.

It was in the small hours of one morning in May that he received orders from Tel Aviv to inquire into the fate of the missing Corporal Devir. As it happened, he found some difficulty, for the first time, in picking up the ciphered message and had to ask Tel Aviv for a repeat. He was given the soldier's name and age, and asked to find out whether he was in Syria, alive or dead.

He knew what the inquiry was about, since he occasionally ventured to listen to the Arabic broadcasts of Kol Israel, the Israeli Radio, though he did not go so far as to tune into the Hebrew broadcasts from Jerusalem. In this way he had learnt that the young corporal was missing and that the Syrians denied all knowledge of him.

Throughout the rest of his time in Syria Cohen concerned

himself with the fate of the missing man, and pursued his inquiries at every opportunity, just as he had been asked to do. But his efforts over the course of three years produced no result: Corporal Devir seemed to have vanished into thin air.

The first occasion that Cohen seized was a conversation he had with Maazi Zahreddin on the verandah of Sheikh el-Ard's country house, some miles out of Damascus. He went to visit the Sheikh, who was a well-known character in the city, with Zahreddin and Alheshan. The Sheikh treated Cohen-Taabes's friends with every courtesy, the one being a military man and the other quite a social figure; they, for their part, were certainly impressed with their host's friendly attitude towards Elie. As they sat over their coffee and sweetmeats, chatting about generalities, Taabes casually asked Maazi: "And when's our trip to the Israeli frontier coming off?"

The Sheikh, who could see no point whatever in such an outing, broke in: "The Israeli frontier? There are plenty of better trips in Syria than that. What can you see there apart from our troops?" Taabes quietly said that he'd like to take a look at the enemy, and Maazi said he would take him to the frontier the following Friday.

So on the Friday Cohen-Taabes set off in the Syrian Army car which belonged to the Chief of Staff's nephew, to inspect the Syrian defence works overlooking Israeli territory on the shores of the Sea of Galilee. As they drove along, Maazi explained that they could tour all the positions except Nukeib. He explained that Nukeib had been closed and declared a top security military area, as the fortifications were being rebuilt.

The frontier was a good 60 miles from Damascus, and Taabes asked all manner of questions on the way about the fighting at Nukeib. Maazi was very excited about the spoils of war that the Syrians had won, especially the Israeli armoured vehicles, which he said were almost undamaged and could now be used by the Syrian Army.

Among the questions that Taabes raised without making a special point of it was "What happened to the Israeli prisoners?" Maazi, in astonishment, asked "What prisoners? We took no prisoners in Nukeib."

This answer was quite sincere, but Taabes went on to ask how the Syrians could have failed to take prisoners in a battle of this kind. Maazi replied: "I wasn't there, but to the best of my knowledge not a single man was captured." The conversation turned to other matters.

After a two-hour drive they got to the top of the hills overlooking the Syrian side of the Sea of Galilee. From there a narrow but usable road zigzags down the barren, rocky slopes from the high ground. There were small tents pitched here and there along the route, especially at crossroads, to provide shade for the soldiers manning the road-blocks. Maazi got through nearly all these without even showing his pass; his lieutenant's shoulder-badges were enough to raise the barriers. Only once was he asked for his papers, which he had ready in the glove-compartment of the car. Leaning over to the sentry and pointing to Cohen-Taabes, he whispered mysteriously: "The gentleman with me is on special duty" – and the barrier went up.

The spy kept his eyes open and made a mental note of everything he saw, knowing that the chance of such a close-up view of the Syrian defence works would not readily come his way again. He was particularly startled to see Russian-made 122-millimetre mortars in position high up on the western flank of the Syrian hills. These weapons, with a range of 12 miles, had just come from the Soviet Union; it was thanks to them that the Syrians had been able to cover a large part of the Jordan Valley with sustained shelling when the Battle of Nukeib broke out. During the frontier tour with Maazi Zahreddin he counted 80 mortars of this type. Israel, he knew, had nothing comparable at that time.

The Spy from Israel and the Chief of Staff's nephew then

visited the fortified area of Kuneitra, where the Syrian District Command is located. From there Cohen got a view of the celebrated Bnot-Yaakov bridge which links the Syrian bank of the Jordan to the Israeli side, but in effect separates the two countries. Naazi stopped the car less than a mile from the Israeli bank and handed Taabes his field-glasses.

"Now you can see the Zionists," he said. "Look, those are their cars and a tractor. Down there is their kibbutz, Mishmar-Hayarden. Easy enough to hit them from here, if you're a good shot." He went on: "I must say that their houses look pretty good, and there are some attractive girls in shorts. Take a look."

Cohen gazed at this peaceful corner of his country. On this hot May afternoon he had a better understanding than before of the Syrian feeling of superiority to Israel, spread out at their feet. The Israeli defences, their kibbutzim, their roads on the other side of the river, lay under direct fire from the Syrian mortars sited above them in the hills.

He could not refrain from remarking to his Syrian guide: "What would be the point of firing from here on those girls or the children of the kibbutz? We ought to be fighting the Israeli Army. Shooting at that sort of target is beneath the dignity of our Army."

But Maazi held another view, widely shared: "Every Israeli, without exception, is a soldier – not just those serving in the Army. A kibbutz is a fortress, to be destroyed like any other military position. Even those girls over there exposing their thighs are soldiers – enemy soldiers."

From Kuneitra they moved off towards Nukeib without touching the forbidden position. Through the windscreen they could see the wonderful landscape of the Jordan valley, the Sea of Galilee, and a dozen kibbutzim dotted about the plain and girded by hills and mountains. Cohen knew every corner of this part of Israel – the town of Tiberias, the kibbutz of Degania with its banana-groves and carp-breeding ponds and, merging into the distance along the west bank of the Jordan, the fields of the kibbutzim of Massada and Ashdot-Yaakov. He had made one of his last trips in Israel in just this area. Now he was seeing it from a Syrian viewpoint.

Maazi Zahreddin made for the little village of Kursi, right on the edge of the Sea of Galilee and a mile and a quarter from the kibbutz of Ein-Gev, which had been so badly damaged in the fighting round Nukeib. Kursi was a typical Arab village of mud houses, their thick walls painted ochre or sky-blue. Syrian soldiers in bathing trunks were lounging by the water's edge.

A few hundred yards away Cohen could see some fishing-boats, Israelis no doubt, since it was here that they usually lowered their nets. There was a general atmosphere of peace and quiet, but he had good reason to survey this landscape with a tightening of the heart. He knew that Soviet mortars were permanently trained on targets in Israel: he had seen them himself.

They sat down in a tin-roofed shanty which served as restaurant and coffee-house. As is usual in Arab coffee-houses, other customers started talking to them quite naturally. The villagers asked the strangers for news from Damascus and remarked on the constant tension in their own area since the Nukeib affair.

An old man busy lighting his *narghileh* (hubble-bubble) remarked that firing on fishermen did no good and should be stopped. "We shoot at them, and they knock Nukeib to bits and go on fishing just as they did before, while we get scared to death. What's the good of it all?" The rest of the company seemed to agree with him.

Maazi told him off for his "defeatist" views. "What have you got to fear from the Zionists? They took a beating at Nukeib," he said. But to Cohen's astonishment the old boy was not going to be put in his place. "Who took a beating? Who won?" he growled. "The Zionists went for Nukeib and took it, and they left three of their half-tracks there. That's the truth!"

Cohen took advantage of the sudden lull to hold forth in a challenging tone: "*We* won at Nukeib, not the Zionists, and we took prisoners, too."

"Dear brother, Nukeib is no distance from here," said another man at the table. "We know the whole story. There wasn't one Zionist taken prisoner, but we know how many of our own men were killed and wounded."

The same thing happened at other Arab military posts and villages in the Nukeib area where they stopped that day. Nothing was known of Zionist prisoners. If it was true that Corporal Devir was in Syrian hands, he must be in some secret place under guard.

Cohen had opportunity later to make repeated inquiries about the missing soldier. He paid visits to frontier villages alone or with Maazi, and he even questioned the staff of Syrian military hospitals and prisons. Right up to the day of his own execution Cohen never solved the riddle of the missing Israeli corporal. It is still a complete mystery. Was Corporal Devir captured by Syrian troops at Nukeib or wasn't he? Was he tortured and hidden away? Is he dead and buried in Syria? No one knows the answer, but in Israel everyone fears the worst.

Cohen got back to Damascus that Friday night with a mass of information, and hurried to his flat opposite the Staff Headquarters. There he rapidly made notes on what he had seen along the frontier – the gun-sites, the type of mortar, the layout of the strong points, the positioning of tanks (of an obsolete German type) near Kuneitra and Kursi, and the number of Soviet recoilless guns. He drafted a written report and, as usual, ciphered it mentally, sending it over the air to Tel Aviv at transmission time.

A few months later, during a brief trip home, he compiled a detailed account of his outing with Maazi Zahreddin. He could not resist adding a few lines to his full description of what he had seen. These supplementary paragraphs tell us more about the sensitive character of Elie Cohen than any posthumous tribute.

"Looking across from Kuneitra at the Valley of Huleh, and standing at Kursi, with the Sea of Galilee and the town of Tiberias before me, I was struck by the tragic folly of this unceasing war between Syria and Israel. The Syrian villagers made me think of the people of Tiberias; they seemed so alike. I told myself then that only the poisonous propaganda concocted by one Syrian Government after another in the past fifteen years prevents the villagers on either side of the lake, Syrians and Israelis, from finding a common language.

"There was only one thing I wanted: it was to seize a boat, cross the water and come home. I was longing to embrace my wife and my little girl, and meet my friends of the Mossad again. I could smell the cornfields of Israel, and felt that the scents of Tel Aviv were being wafted to me by the breeze.

"But our little lake, the Sea of Galilee, became a vast and terrible ocean: it completely separated me from my country. My isolation then seemed to me a necessary evil. I felt like a lighthouse desperately passing its warning signals through the night, signals to save the ship called Israel from the dangers that were threatening it."

An official of the Israeli Secret Service copied out these paragraphs and had them stencilled for circulation to the heads of the main departments. They came from "an unnamed agent".

14

A FRESH BRIEFING

Elie Cohen had spent some six months in Damascus when he received orders over his radio to return to Israel for a short spell. He was to seize the first opportunity to leave for Europe and move on from there.

Things had been pretty quiet in Damascus during the summer of 1962. The internal political situation had, up to a point, settled down, and there had been no striking incidents on the border with Israel. A few days after getting his orders from Tel Aviv, he told his friends Alheshan and Maazi that he proposed to take a brief business trip to Europe – a prospect that they envied him. It was certainly pleasanter to be in Switzerland or Germany (where he told them he was going) for part of the summer than to spend it in Syria under a blazing sun where the temperature could average 40° C. in the shade.

He made the now familiar round of a dozen dealers in Syrian *objets d'art*, asking them for samples that he could market in Europe. Salinger in Zurich had armed him with letters to confirm that he intended to import Syrian furniture; so Cohen also ordered some Shesh-Besh tables, complete with gaming boards, and despatched the lot to the address of the import-export firm in Zurich that he was supposed to be representing in Syria.

Some days before he left, he heard from Maazi Zahreddin that one of his Buenos Aires acquaintances, General el-Hafez, the former Military Attaché, was back in Damascus and looking for a job at Staff Headquarters. Maazi knew him well, and offered to bring them together, but Taabes, thanking Maazi, said he preferred to postpone the meeting until his return from Europe.

He booked his air-passage to Zurich and Munich. On his way home from the travel agency he passed a small shop in the centre of Damascus that specialised in Syrian Army uniforms and the badges and insignia of its different units. Making sure that no one else was in the shop, he went in, and told the owner that he had just opened a souvenir shop in Aleppo, and would like to stock up with military badges and decorations, for which he thought he could find a sale.

The shopkeeper was delighted at the chance of doing a deal with this supposed provincial. He asked whether his visitor could pay cash, and produced the official catalogue of badges and medals in use in the Syrian Army. Cohen wanted to buy the catalogue "so as to study it at leisure and send you my orders from Aleppo". There was the usual haggle over the price, which ended in Cohen leaving the shop with the catalogue under his arm. As soon as he got home, he cut out the pages showing the distinctive unit badges, hid them carefully in his suitcase, and threw away the rest of the catalogue.

He radioed Tel Aviv that he was off to Europe the next day. In his flat, which he double-locked, he left his transmitter, hidden in its usual place. As no one had discovered it during the six months that he had been using it almost every day, there was no reason to fear that it would be discovered in his absence.

He caught the plane from Damascus, and spent thre days in Zurich without making any contacts. Once he was sure that he was not being followed, he booked a seat for Munich, where he at once got in touch with Salinger, his "business" link – and the principal European contact of the Israel Secret Service.

Salinger, who had been warned of his coming, had in his office one of the tables from Damascus that Cohen had sent off some days earlier. "The other table is already at Tel Aviv", Salinger told him, and he added, with a wink, "Our friends are going to work out the best use we can make of it."

He helped Cohen buy presents for his wife and little girl and various relatives, took back the Syrian clothes in exchange for the ones Cohen had last brought from Israel, and gave him back his Israeli passport. It was arranged that post-cards Cohen had written should be sent off later to his friends in Damascus. The two men also agreed on the text of the business letters to be sent to the Damascus dealers, confirming orders.

Six days after he had left Damascus, Elie Cohen was back in Israel. He was moved to tears, as he passed through the Israeli controls at Lydda airport, to hear Hebrew spoken all round him again. The customs took no interest in reproductions of Syrian badges and medals that he had cut out of the catalogue. But he had to pay duty on the toys he was taking his little girl.

A young man he didn't know beckoned to him as he left the customs, and showed him into a private car. In the back seat was Yitzhak the Dervish, who clasped his former pupil round the shoulders in a warm embrace. They hardly talked at all as they drove to Tel Aviv. However, Elie told the Dervish that he had a present for him in his suitcase, but the Dervish replied that his best present was to have him back.

Nadia and Sophie had no idea at all that Elie was arriving out of the blue, and were overcome with joy to see him. He had been given three clear days' leave at home before he set foot in the Secret Service Headquarters, and it took him only a few hours to get used to being Elie Cohen again, with his Kamal Taabes' personality temporarily put on ice. The whole Cohen family welcomed him back and, as on the previous visit, he excused his long absence by the demands of a business that was expanding in Europe.

When he got down to work, he drafted report after report, setting down everything he knew about the politics, economy and armed forces of Syria in the fullest detail. He was given a file of all the messages he had sent off from his bedroom in Damascus during the past six months, which made it easier to put events in their chronological order.

The Dervish, whose office was next to the room in which Cohen was working, jumped for joy when his young friend handed over the special present from Damascus – the catalogue of military badges. Here was fresh evidence of the initiative and daring of the Spy from Israel.

With a colleague, the Dervish, who had been Cohen's direct control throughout, questioned him during the next few days on a number of points in his report. They wanted to know everything – personal particulars of the officers and prominent personalities that the spy had met in Damascus; additional details of the frontier villages and defence works; the political balance of power inside Syria, and the prospects of various officers and leaders. The questions ranged from the price of sugar in Damascus to the state of public morale. All the conversations were recorded on tape and circulated to other branches of the Secret Service.

Cohen then had expert instruction in a new cipher system, which was to replace the old one for security reasons. His chiefs were anxious, again for security reasons, that he should find a different hiding-place for his transmitter, as they thought there must be a better place than the hole in the ceiling. He rejected this suggestion, claiming that he had found the ideal spot in his flat, which no one would ever discover. On the other hand, his set might break down, so he asked for a second one.

The detailed account that he had given of the different trends in the Syrian Government and Army strengthened the conviction of his chiefs that Cohen, apart from settling down wonderfully in Damascus, was keeping himself *au fait* with events, and could form an accurate assessment of how the internal situation would evolve.

Accordingly, they briefed him on the main problem which was troubling the Government of Israel at the time, and which would inevitably affect the frontier position. This was the fulfilment of the Government's scheme to divert the waters of the Jordan from the Sea of Galilee and direct them to the South of Israel. The Syrian attacks in the Tiberias area and the mortar-fire across the Sea of Galilee had not been aimed so much against the fishermen as against the principle of Israel's territorial sovereignty there. For it was from the Sea of Galilee that fresh water was intended to pass through an extensive network of canals to the Negev Desert in the South.

The Syrians were trying, in brief, to invalidate, in practice if not in theory, Israel's rights over the waters. They were seeking to maintain a state of tension in this area, come what may, so as to thwart the Israelis' tremendous plans for the development of the country's desert regions.

As the Dervish told Cohen, the scheme had already cost Israel 250 million Israeli pounds, and a further 400 million pounds was due to be spent before 1962 was over. Thus it was vital for the Cabinet to know whether the Syrians' threat to damage Israel by diverting the sources of the Jordan, i.e. its tributaries the Banias and Hasbani rivers,* was based on a real

* The third tributary, the Dan, rose in Israeli territory. The Banias rises in the Golan Heights, and thus since 1967 has been in an Israeli controlled area. The original Arab scheme was to divert the Hasbani into the Litani which flows into the Mediterranean through the southern Lebanon, and to divert the Banias into the Yarmuk which is in Jordanian territory.

concrete programme. If it proved true that the Syrians could interfere with the headwaters of the Jordan, the Sea of Galilee would fall to a level that would make it impossible to draw on it to irrigate the Negev desert, and the whole Water Carrier system would be placed in jeopardy.

In these circumstances, said the Dervish, the most urgent task for the Israeli Government's man in Damascus related to Syrian plans in this field. Any information, however scrappy, that he could get out of Damascus could from now on prove decisive to the Israeli appreciation of Syrian strategy. It should therefore have priority over any other inquiry. In other words, his principal job would be to investigate any Syrian schemes for diverting the waters of the Jordan, as well as any attempt to sabotage Israeli designs. With the maps before him, he was briefed on details of the Syrian plan, showing where the Banias and Hasbani rivers rose, and told the technical methods that the Syrians might use to wreck Israel's future.

Shortly before he was due to go back to Syria, he was startled to get back from the Dervish the top part of the Shesh-Besh table – the actual gaming-board sent on from Munich by Salinger. The Dervish took a sharp-bladed knife such as shoe-makers use and, with a flick of the wrist, dismantled the bottom of the drawer underneath the board, in which the players normally keep their pieces. The two layers of wood that formed the false bottom of the drawer would be ideal for hiding micro-films and other minute documents. He demonstrated how to take the two layers apart with a penknife, and how to glue them together with a special adhesive after inserting the micro-film. "Whenever you use a Shesh-Besh board for sending us documents," he said, "give us a radio warning 'Parcel Des-patched,' and we'll do what's needed."

The spy was provided with the second miniature trans-mitter he had asked for, and a German camera to supplement the Japanese one he had in Damascus. He could no doubt have got from his chiefs as much money as he cared to suggest. All he asked for from the Dervish was 650 francs (then approximately £50) "just for once, to buy presents for my friends in Damascus." His instructor was surprised at such a modest request, but Elie maintained that it would be sufficient for all the presents he had to get.

Saying good-bye to Nadia, he told her: "I don't know when I'll be back, but you'll certainly see me as soon as I know that you're having another child – and I'd prefer a boy this time."

He left for Damascus about the end of July 1962. Israeli agents elsewhere had just launched a major campaign against the German scientists working in Cairo. For the tenth anniversary of his accession, on July 21, Nasser had taken Israel and the world by surprise by parading through the streets of Cairo the first guided missiles made in Egypt, with the help of scientists who, eighteen years earlier, had been working for the Nazis in Germany.

15

SURPRISE PARTY AND SURPRISE COUP

Cohen gave a party in his flat to celebrate his return to Damascus. This is how he met a man who held a senior post in the Syrian Ministry at Propaganda and Information. His name was George Seif, and at 32 he was already Head of the Radio and Press Sections, where it was his job to see that political news was slanted to make public opinion favourable to the authorities.

The party brought together all Cohen's Syrian friends, among them Kamal Alheshan, Maazi Zahreddin and Sheikh el-Ard, as well as various businessmen whom he had cultivated before his European trip. He presented Maazi with an array of silk ties with labels from the best shops in Paris and Rome. His presents for Kamal Alheshan, from Hermes in Paris, were a handsome red leather desk set and blotter to match, stamped with his initials.

It was Alheshan who had brought along George Seif and the young woman with him. Seif seemed anxious to hear the latest from Paris, but not about foreign affairs. Like Maazi and Alheshan, he wanted the most recent gay Parisian gossip – all the titbits about the Pigalle nightclub and the strip-tease scandals. All these young Syrians had been around in the

Lebanese "hot spots", and were enthralled by the stories that Taabes, who had never in his life set foot in such establishments in Paris or Munich, invented for their benefit.

As for the businessmen, the spy promised them the earth after his European tour. He told them that there was every chance of their mutual interests working out well. "I'm so confident," he told them, "that I propose to put my own money into this business. There's definitely a market in Western Europe for our arts and crafts." Somehow or other, he knew, Salinger would dispose of everything he was sent.

Seif followed their bright conversation with interest. He, too, was a lively young man, who spoke several European languages, and he was evidently delighted to meet Taabes. He was full of admiration for his flat, his style of living and his trips to Europe. He even liked the way Taabes himself served coffee to the dozen friends that he was entertaining, though he asked one rather awkward question. "How is it," he asked, "that a man of your standing doesn't engage a servant? Wouldn't it suit you to have a woman to do the housework and the cooking?"

Cohen-Taabes had good reasons for not having a woman to do the housework. He gave Seif a wink and said, "If I take on a woman for housework, I shall never get married. The first woman I bring in here will be my wife, one of our lovely young Syrian girls."

Seif turned the conversation to his own job at the Ministry. "My work," he said, "is mainly journalism. I have to attend all the official functions, but I have the free run of practically all Government Departments and I'm in the good books of all our Ministers." He turned to the young woman – his assistant, Reit el-Houli – for confirmation of his boast.

Luck again favoured the spy. Through his connections in Damascus he eventually became very friendly with George Seif, to whom he confessed that he had always cherished an admiration for journalists, who managed to be everywhere at once and know everyone and everything. He had wanted to become one himself, but (he added with a hint of chagrin) "I'm just a passable businessman, I'm afraid."

"If you'd like to get a better idea of my work," said Seif, "look in on me during working hours. Here's my card." Taabes thanked him effusively and promised to call on him at the Ministry.

As soon as his friends had gone, he took the reserve transmitter he had brought back from Europe and hid it away, wrapped in a piece of waterproof material to keep out dust and damp, in the cavity of the mechanism operating the shutter of his sitting-room window, facing the Staff Headquarters.

A week after their first meeting, he called on Seif at the Ministry of Information, where he was made welcome and introduced to the young man's colleagues. Over a coffee in the Ministry canteen Cohen-Taabes happened to mention Argentina and his Syrian friends there, dropping the name of General el-Hafez, the former Military Attaché, now back in Syria.

Seif said that he knew him well; indeed, he was a friend of his. When Taabes remarked that he would like to say 'how do you do' to the General and welcome him back, Seif promised to arrange a meeting: "Nothing easier". He was as good as his word, and before the week was out Taabes was knocking at the General's front door, no distance from where he himself lived in the fashionable Abu-Rumana district.

General el-Hafez, who had returned to active politics in the Baath party since he had got back to Damascus, did not immediately recall the name of Kamal Amin Taabes, "the Syrian from Buenos Aires" whom George Seif had mentioned favourably. But when the well-dressed businessman sitting in the General's drawing-room thanked him warmly for having advised him, in Buenos Aires, to go back to Syria, he remembered.

"As a mark of gratitude for your valuable advice," said

Taabes, "I've taken the liberty of bringing you a small gift"; and he held out to the General (whom he remembered as a pipe-smoker) a large tin of good tobacco that he had bought in Germany. He spoke to the General about his plans for exporting Syrian *objets d'art* to Europe, and also told him that he had it in mind to start campaigning in Argentina to persuade Syrians out there to make profitable investments in their mother-country.

The General, plainly overwhelmed by his visitor's charm, tact and enthusiasm, congratulated him on his efforts and demonstrated the warmth of his regard by finally addressing him as "Ya Ahi" (My Brother). Their conversation ranged far and wide, and el-Hafez expressed his anxiety about Syria's internal problems, remarking that there was only one party (meaning the Baath) that could save the country.

He saw Taabes to the door with the words "Let my home be yours" – a common Arab expression. Taabes nevertheless felt that it sealed the success of his first visit to the General, who was shortly to rise to the supreme office of President of the Syrian Arab Republic. Meanwhile his visit to el-Hafez and to the Ministry of Information provided material for a number of cipher messages to Tel Aviv.

His meetings with Seif became more and more frequent. So often did he call at his office that eventually the doorkeepers at the Ministry knew him by sight and let him into the building without asking for his identity card. Seif had become the spy's friend and companion more rapidly, and on more intimate terms, than Alheshan or Maazi. Seif spent hours in his flat, telling him endless tales and anecdotes about the régime. These were incorporated in the messages to Tel Aviv.

It was, for instance, from Seif that he learned that a Syrian deputation had been in the U.S.S.R. to ask the Soviet Government for help in diverting the waters of the Hasbani. According to Seif, Moscow had not declined the proposal, but was in no great hurry to act on it.

Meanwhile Seif's responsibilities at the Ministry of Information were extended. He was given general political supervision over the foreign broadcasts of Damascus Radio, and the promotion of his new friend was soon to prove of special importance for Taabes.

George Seif, who had a decided weakness for a number of young women, indulged in illicit escapades extremely risky for anyone in his public position. On these jaunts he often went about with Colonel Salim Hatoum, who commanded the shock troops – the crack paratroopers of the Syrian Army.

Early in the autumn of 1962 Seif, who was by now firmly attached to the spy and saw him two or three times a week, suggested organising an intimate "surprise party" at Kamal Taabes's flat with Colonel Hatoum and two or three girls they knew. Cohen said he would be delighted, and the party was held – though it was rather innocent, actually. George Seif had brought his secretary, Rcita cl-Huli, a plump young Syrian girl with black hair and gleaming eyes who was really in love with her boss. Colonel Hatoum's companion was a minor employee of the Turkish Embassy in Damascus.

At the beginning of the party Hatoum was rather reserved. He didn't know Taabes and was on his guard. If his intrigue should leak out, he might lose his Army appointment and his rank. But Cohen-Taabes made great efforts to flatter the Colonel, a brawny, hefty-looking fellow, highly conscious of his exalted status. When several hours had passed and the host had plied his very private guests with brandy and whisky, the ice was broken, and Colonel Hatoum obviously felt more at ease.

The spy made up his mind to do things in style so as to keep these private parties going in his flat. The day after the first party he bought a record-player and a batch of slow, sentimental dance records. He took the earliest opportunity of telling George Seif that he had greatly enjoyed their evening together and that his flat was available at any time for amorous frolics both to Seif and to Hatoum, whom he referred to as "our handsome friend".

The intimate gatherings became a habit, which lasted through the winter of 1962–3. Seif and Hatoum availed themselves of Taabes's hospitality at least once a fortnight. They would invite two or three girl-friends and had some quite pleasant evenings in Abu-Rumana.

Cohen filled the glasses, changed the records, and occasionally danced with one of the girls, but he had made it an unbreakable rule not to get involved with any of them, but to keep things just on a friendly footing. Concentrated as he was on his duties, the spy had obvious reasons for remaining a spectator, and lending a ready ear to any remarks that might come from the Syrian Colonel or the civil servant. They were both well briefed about the country.

Colonel Hatoum made no bones about speaking his mind on the men in power in Syria: "A timid, flabby lot," he would say, when he got lit up by the drink. "They're all terrified of Israel, shivering in their pants. It's time for a change." Then, as if he wanted to prove what a powerful army Syria had, he would reel off its military inventory: "Two Armoured Divisions, five Infantry Divisions, four fighter squadrons. But my shock troops are worth more than the rest of the Army put together. The boys under my orders are tough and well trained: they've got no reason to be afraid of the Zionists, and they're ready to give their lives for their country."

In December 1962 the Syrians resumed hostilities against Israel. They had made good the damage to their fortified position at Nukeib, and from here they opened fire on Israelis fishing in the Sea of Galilee. At the same time, farm-workers at the Tel Katzir kibbutz were fired on from other Syrian positions, while ploughing a narrow strip along the disputed frontier. Further north, near the River Dan, the only tributary of the Jordan that rises from a source inside Israel, the Syrians made an attack on an Army patrol the same day.

Elie Cohen sent message after message to Tel Aviv. That winter he was ciphering despatches two or three times the length of those he had sent early in 1962. He had a mass of information to cope with, all of it gathered from good sources – Maazi Zahreddin, George Seif, Colonel Hatoum – to say nothing of news he picked up himself on the fringe of civilian politics. What he sent was at once passed on by Tel Aviv to the Army and the Prime Minister.

The situation was coming to the boil again. Either side was liable to launch a major operation. Ben-Gurion, addressing Israeli armoured units in the Negev on December 11, issued a clear warning:

"Tsahal (The Israeli Army) will strike its Syrian enemy wherever that enemy is to be found: on the hills overlooking the Sea of Galilee, in their fortified positions, and even at certain points that they imagine to be out of our reach. I warn the Government in Damascus: hands off our farmworkers and peaceful villages!"

During the next few days the whole frontier area was soaked by rainstorms, and this seems to have caused a holdup in Syrian military operations. However, on December 20 Cohen sent the following message from Damascus: "Colonel Ziad el-Hariri, commanding troops stationed along our frontier, is pressing Damascus for operational all-clear. Damascus is hesitant, fearing a riposte."

Acting on this message, the Israeli Army proclaimed a state of alert throughout the Northern Zone. The next day, a small piece of evidence indicated that Damascus was definitely withdrawing its challenge. The tractor-drivers of Tel Katzir took advantage of the first sunshine, after several rainy days, to start ploughing their fields on the frontier again. This time not a shot came from Syria to interrupt their work. Damascus was aware of the alert in the Northern Zone of Israel and had given the troops strict orders not to create an incident.

A new phase in the relations between Cohen and his friends George Seif and Colonel Salim Hatoum began on Christmas Eve. Over lunch that day Seif lowered his voice and asked for a favour:

"Hatoum and I really enjoy our parties at your flat," he said, "and we are most grateful. But seeing that you yourself never take an active part in the fun, couldn't you sometimes let us have the key of your flat – in the daytime, you know, at mid-day or between five and seven? Of course, we'll clear up after-wards. What about it?"

Cohen agreed. It was arranged that on the days it was needed, the key of his flat should be left in his letter-box, which would be open. Seif had simply to ring him up in the morning and say that he or Hatoum wanted the use of the flat during the day. This was the least return that the spy could make to his principal sources of information.

Meanwhile Cohen did not neglect his export business. During December the first sizeable consignment of Damascus tables, local leatherwork and costumes left for Europe via Beirut, and from now on there were regular shipments. The consignee in Munich or Zurich (Cohen's "resident director", Salinger) was thus enabled to send him sums of money that naturally amounted to more than he had to pay his local suppliers. Thus the funds needed to finance the spy's work reached him through a convincingly businesslike transaction.

His discreet acceptance of the fairly frequent visits that Seif and Hatoum (with companions) made to his flat when he was not there gained him their complete confidence. Hatoum let him know that a rising against the civilian Cabinet in Damascus was being promoted at Staff Headquarters by Colonel Ziad el-Hariri, the commander of the front-line troops. This

officer of only 37, who came from Hama, was in complete control
of the divisions stationed on the Israeli frontier.

Cohen was given this news in February 1963, and he
conveyed to Tel Aviv over his secret radio the first intimation of
a probable *coup d'état*. The original message spells out the
name of his informant, Colonel Salim Hatoum.*

This valuable piece of Intelligence was closely scrutinised
by the Secret Service experts in Tel Aviv, who were quite used to
getting reliable reports from their agent in Damascus, but
decided on this occasion that he was passing on current local
rumours of no immediate consequence. However, a month
later, during the night of March 8–9, 1963, the *coup d'état* that
Hatoum's indiscretion had enabled Cohen to predict duly took
place.

Instead of proceeding to Amman, where the Damascus
Government, having got wind of his intentions, had posted him
as Military Attaché, Colonel Ziad el-Hariri had provided troops
to cover the coup. At a press conference called in Tel Aviv on
Saturday evening, March 9, General Meir Amit, the Head of

---

* Cohen never knew that Salim Hatoum had a younger brother, Faris
Hatoum, whose career was very different. They belonged to a rich and respectable Druse family from the mountainous region of Jebel Druse, extending
over the border from Syria into Jordan – the home of the magnificent Druse
tribesmen. The Hatoum family background was conservative and military, and
both brothers were destined for a military career in Syria. However,
Faris soon became disillusioned by the haughty attitude of his Moslem
seniors. In 1947 he found his way into Palestine, where he was fired with
enthusiasm for the struggle of the Jews against the British Mandate, and
joined the Haganah (Jewish Defence organisation). The following year,
during Israel's War of Independence, he conducted several espionage operations for Israel inside Syria. Later, as an Israeli officer, he commanded a
detachment of troops drawn from Israel's Druse minority, who had
volunteered for Army service.

In 1950 Faris Hatoum was accepted as a convert to Judaism by the
Rabbinate of Tel Aviv. He married a young Jewess, by whom he has four
children. Their household in Israel keeps to a strictly Kosher diet. After
1947 Faris did not see his brother Salim again.

Israeli Military Intelligence, was able to provide Israeli journalists with this information.

The Prime Minister of Israel, Mr. Ben-Gurion, who was again spending his Saturday at the Galei Kinneret hotel on the Sea of Galilee, was less troubled by the previous day's excitement in Damascus than by the problems created by the arrest of two Israeli agents in Switzerland. These two men – Joseph Ben-Gal, an Israeli subject, and Otto Joklik, an Austrian working for Israel – had been trying to secure the withdrawal from Egypt of a member of the team of German scientists, Professor Goerke. They hoped to manage this through pressure on his daughter Heidi.

Goerke was at the time the most mysterious and, in Israeli eyes, most dangerous figure at the notorious "Base 333" at Helwan on the Nile south of Cairo, where a top-secret military programme was being implemented by a predominantly German scientific staff, and Goerke himself was in charge of the production of guided missiles for Nasser.

The two agents had met Fräulein Goerke in a hotel in Basle, but in a matter of hours the co-operation of the Egyptian and German Secret Service with the Swiss Police had brought about their arrest in Zurich, where they were thrown into prison. Ben-Gurion's first step was to request the Swiss Government to release them.

Their arrest caused such an international scandal that Ben-Gurion resolved to bring to an end the anti-German campaign of the Israeli Secret Service directed by Isser Harel. It had not managed to stop Goerke and twenty other scientists and technicians entering Nasser's employment. On April 1, 1963, Isser Harel resigned (as related in an earlier chapter), telling Ben-Gurion: "You'll have to find another Secret Service chief to carry out your new policy."

The resignation of "Little Isser" was a serious loss to the Secret Service and disturbed some of his closest colleagues, but his successor, who has continued to direct the Secret Service up to the present time, on lines different from Harel's, has given a new impetus to this vital branch of Defence. However, the repercussions of this affair worried the Israeli Government for some weeks, just when Syria was preoccupied with its own internal worries following the coup.

A Government quite unlike its predecessors had come into power in Syria, and it opened up a new phase in the country's existence and, incidentally, a new phase for the spy from Israel. His friend Colonel Salim Hatoum had taken a leading part in the March 9 coup. Using his commando units, he had seized the Staff Headquarters building opposite Cohen's windows in a dawn assault, and occupied Damascus Radio station.

These changes propelled Cohen right into the centre of the group that had brought them about. More to the point, he was closely involved with the private lives of the heroes who had just stepped in to control their country's future. Colonel Salim Hatoum had hardly completed his brisk take-over of power than he was on the phone to his friend Taabes, asking to borrow his flat for his Turkish girl-friend and himself. "I want," he said, "to hold a victory celebration!" However, the revolution was not entirely to the spy's advantage as it had resulted in the dismissal of General Abdel Karim Zahreddin, Commander-in-Chief and Minister of Defence, the uncle of his friend Maazi.

After the coup the Baath party took political control of Syria, the Premiership going to Salah el-Bitar, a former leader of the party, which provided twelve of the twenty Ministers. Some days later the Syrian Baath and its fraternal Baath party of Iraq sent a joint deputation to Egypt, and the three countries signed a mutual assistance pact in Cairo on April 17.

However, experts regarded this pact as a poor camouflage for a deep rift between Damascus and Cairo. While proclaiming its highest regard for Nasser and Arab national unity, the Baath was very far from wanting to repeat its unhappy experience during the abortive Union of Egypt and Syria. The party's primary object was to assure Syria's independence, whether this was compatible with good relations with Egypt or not.

Elie Cohen passed on his observations and conclusions to his organisation at Tel Aviv; he also provided full information about the new masters of Damascus. But the position was wrongly interpreted by Ben-Gurion, who disregarded his agent's guidance, and took at its face value the three-nation pact hastily signed between Egypt, Syria and Iraq. He sent off letters to President Kennedy and General de Gaulle, among others, expressing his anxiety in face of this new threat, and asked for their support against this danger to Israel's future.

However, before Ben-Gurion could get a reply from the statesmen to whom he had appealed, the three-nation pact was already in fragments. The new turn in events was conveyed by Elie Cohen in a message he sent on April 27.

"Baath taking vigorous action against pro-Nasser officers. Two regiments loyal to Chief of Staff Colonel Hariri just paraded through city streets. Arrest of officers known for pro-Nasser sympathies imminent. General el-Hafez in charge of operations. His influence with Baath predominant."

A spy's career is apt to have curious twists. El-Hafez, the man who at Buenos Aires had advised Elie Cohen to go back to Syria and, more recently, congratulated him on his initiative in exporting to Europe, was one of those who profited from the Baath's rise to power. He was now Minister of the Interior in the new Government, and was thus at this stage responsible for Syria's Counter-espionage Service. Elie Cohen, too, had been swept along by events beyond his control, and found himself pushed closer and closer into the circle of Syria's ruling few. At the end of April he sent General el-Hafez a bouquet of flowers with his congratulations.

Some weeks after this, in mid-May, Cohen's friends

arranged a huge party in his flat, which two years later was to figure in Syrian history as the "Orgy of the Revolution". George Seif and a few others were there, with a number of Syrian girls. The party began with toasts to the "Victory of Baath"; it ended in the most unbridled orgy.

Cohen had to keep a grip on himself not to get drunk, as his friends did. He alone had to stay awake and in control of his senses until the next morning. In addition to his normal reasons for keeping clear of his friends' amorous exploits, this time there was a special inducement: Colonel Salim Hatoum had brought with him another staff officer, Colonel Salah Dalli, whom he introduced to Taabes as the "rising star of Baath".

When his friends left Cohen-Taabes's flat the next morning, it was in complete chaos. But while he was changing his bed sheets, he could glean some satisfaction from the knowledge that in future his friends would think of him as really "one of us".

16

A NAZI IN DAMASCUS

In the course of that spring Elie Cohen found himself on the track of several notorious Nazis who had found a peaceful refuge in the capital of Syria. Chance had been on his side again. One day his friend Sheikh Majd el-Ard confessed to him that not so long ago he had been married to an Egyptian Jewess for a while; this more or less bogus union was her only means of getting a Syrian residence permit. However, the Sheikh, in a confidential mood, went on to say: "It's not that I've any particular liking for Jews. On the contrary. I lived for two years in Hitler's Germany during the Second World War."

He had had an unqualified admiration for the Nazi régime, and was sorry to have to come home when the Third Reich was overthrown.

In his most innocent tones, Taabes asked whether he knew any former Nazis in Damascus, remarking "I'm a passionate reader of books on the war and the Nazi régime."

"Of course I do," said el-Ard. "One of them is my best friend. He has a job as adviser to Syrian Security."

Taabes said he would like to meet the ex-Nazi, so the Sheikh arranged that they should call on him together a few days later. In the Sheikh's Peugeot, they drove across Nabek

Bridge in the centre of Damascus and parked in Shahabandar Street, in front of an attractive house standing in a garden, quite near a leading Syrian bank. On the top floor they were welcomed by an elderly man who looked like a European. His wife was there too.

He introduced himself to Taabes under the name of Rozelli, but the Sheikh cut him short. "My friend here is a man of honour; you can trust him. You needn't be afraid to tell him your real name, Rademacher – Franz Rademacher."

This was a name Elie had never heard, and he couldn't guess what sort of person this was. However, the German himself enlightened him. Though extremely reticent about his present position in Syria, Rozelli-Rademacher grumbled about the ill-luck that had dogged his later years: "The Jews and the Germans are constantly after me. They accuse me, quite wrongly, of having killed Jews during the war. Fortunately, I'm comparatively undisturbed in Damascus and allowed to earn a respectable living."

Bit by bit, he opened out. He was in regular contact with two other ex-Nazis: von Hantke, who had been head of the Arab section of Hitler's Foreign Ministry and was now a political adviser in Saudi Arabia; and the S.S. Colonel Kriebel, who had settled in Damascus at the end of the Second World War and been of considerable service to his Syrian hosts in 1948, at the time of the war with Israel.

The man who was unburdening himself to Taabes looked about fifty, though really he was about ten years older. He had a good physique for his age and, like Cohen himself, had grown an Oriental-looking moustache as part of his disguise. The spy could not believe his ears when he was given all this information about the Nazis. He found out a good deal more before rushing home to send off a message to Tel Aviv:

"Met ex-Nazi Franz Rademacher sixtyish working for Syrian intelligence."

He added details like Rademacher's exact address, his wife's name, and the gist of the information he had got from him, and concluded with the words "Proposing liquidate Rademacher". Next day the reply from Tel Aviv arrived:

"Avoid at all costs any incident regarding R that could risk compromising your main task. Keep watching him and report further. Was one of Eichmann's chief assistants."

It was only then that Cohen learned that he had discovered a major war criminal, whose name had been brought up on several occasions during the Eichmann trial in Jerusalem. The German Police and the Secret Service of more than one country had been looking for Rademacher for ten years, but had lost all trace of him.

Section O6 of the Israeli Police, which had been responsible for interrogating Eichmann before his trial, had established the following facts about Rademacher in 1961: He had been a senior member of the Foreign Ministry under the Third Reich, and had originated the scheme for deporting all European Jews to Madagascar. This scheme had been kept alive by the Nazis up to the time that they resolved to go ahead with the liquidation of the Jews – the grisly plan known as the "Final Solution".

When Eichmann was interrogated in Israel in February 1961, he admitted that Rademacher had telephoned him on September 12, 1941, passing on a suggestion from the German Ambassador in Belgrade that the Jews of Serbia should be deported to Russia. Eichmann thought it preferable to liquidate them on the spot. A long correspondence between Rademacher, in the Foreign Ministry, and Eichmann followed, and finally Eichmann decided to go to Belgrade himself and "organise the liquidation of the Jews of Serbia".

Rademacher was picked up in Germany after the war, and brought before a Federal German court on a charge of assisting in the murder of 1,500 Jews from Belgrade and in the deportation of Belgian Jews to Auschwitz. Before receiving a sentence of a mere three and a half years' imprisonment, he had been released on bail, and seized the chance to escape. He found temporary refuge in Argentina – like so many others – and from that moment all trace of him vanished. His name never came up again until after Eichmann's capture. Now, in 1963, thanks to Elie Cohen, he had been discovered in Damascus.

Later, Cohen learned from something Rozelli-Rademacher let drop that another character likely to interest his "Head Office" in Tel Aviv was living in Syria. A certain Heinrich Springer was engaged (under the name of "Stringer") in arms traffic between several countries in Western Europe and Syria. Springer, whose previous history was vague and obscure, had a meeting with Cohen-Taabes at the Oumaya Hotel in Damascus, but refused to answer questions about his past or his present activities.

On instructions from Tel Aviv, Cohen had to suspend his inquiries among the ex-Nazis in Damascus. More urgent duties bearing on Israel's Defence were to absorb his energies. However, it was not long after his first meeting with Rademacher that the Bonn Government, still looking for this war criminal, received all the relevant information from Jerusalem. The German Ambassador in Damascus was able to follow up the clues they had been given "from an Israeli source" – i.e. Elie Cohen – but it was not until March 1965 that Bonn was able to demand Franz Rademacher's extradition.

17

"HATOUMGRAD"

Throughout the spring of 1963, which brought about such decisive political changes in Syria, the flow of cipher messages between Cohen's flat in Damascus and his "Head Office" in Tel Aviv was uninterrupted. The spy, ideally placed to know the internal intrigues and trends of the new régime, was asked for more and more detailed information, and sent off replies every day at eight in the evening, but sometimes at eight in the morning as well.

On rare occasions he used his transmitter to follow up the few dozen words of the message proper with a sentence or two to be passed to his family. In his despatches of this period, sentences like "Please don't forget Nadia's birthday present" crop up, or "Please send my daughter Sophie some small souvenir from Europe". There was only one occasion that spring when Tel Aviv used its radio contact with Damascus to send its agent a personal message. At the tail of an inquiry about the intentions of the Baath régime towards Israel and the frontier situation came the following words, which were twice repeated: "Nadia expecting a child".

The spy, who had long hoped for a boy, decided that the news required joyful celebration. Normally it would have been an occasion for asking in one's family or friends. His friends in Damascus – genuine and close friends, sincerely attached to Kamal Amin Taabes – were Maazi Zahreddin and George Seif; they could well have been friends of his in quite different circumstances, quite apart from being sources of Intelligence. As soon as he knew that he could expect a second child, he rang up each of them and asked him to dinner. As Seif was already engaged to dine with one of the officials of Damascus Airport, it was arranged that they should all meet there.

This was the happiest evening that Cohen ever spent in Damascus, though his Syrian friends naturally had no idea why he was in such good spirits. Eventually Seif asked him why he was so exuberantly cheerful, and he gave what sounded like a serious answer:

"I'm happy to be able to tell you that I'm on the point of translating one of my most cherished dreams into reality. I'm going back to Argentine to raise some real capital among the Syrians who live in Buenos Aires." He knew that his "Head Office", having told him that his wife was about to have a child, would give him short leave in Israel, when the time came.

Maazi and George congratulated him on his decision, and Seif's friend, Iliya el-Maaz, who turned out to be one of the key men at the airport, joined them in drinking Kamal Amin's health. He was responsible for co-ordinating civil and military traffic at Damascus International Airport, which is used by both civil airlines and the Syrian Air Force. So this dinner, to celebrate an approaching family occasion of which no one except the person concerned was aware, provided Cohen-Taabes with a new friend who was shortly to be an important source of military information.

It was usual at that time for the Syrians to use four Mig 19 fighters daily on sorties above the Israeli border, mainly for the purpose of taking air photographs of the frontier zone. For several weeks these machines operated with clockwork regularity; four Israeli Super-Mystere fighters, made in France, appeared at the edge of Israel's air-space, kept the Migs under observation and, if necessary, drove them off.

Suddenly, without any obvious reason, the Syrians stopped these air manoeuvres. Israeli Military Headquarters was still wondering what had happened – thinking a military problem of this kind inappropriate to put to Cohen – when Cohen, off his own bat, gave the answer.

This was the message he sent:

"Four Mig 19s based Damascus International Airport grounded. One pilot removed for political deviation. Second pilot ill. Third pilot injured in car accident."

Naturally Cohen had got the facts from Iliya el-Maaz, whom he had asked to dinner with George Seif and Maazi Zahreddin. With three pilots out of action, the Syrian Air Force had cancelled the daily reconnaissance flights of the four Migs. The Israeli General Staff at Tel Aviv deduced that if the Syrians could not find replacements for three Mig 19 pilots who were not available for reconnaissance duties, they must have a very limited number of operational pilots. It was a perfectly sound deduction.

A story concerning one of Cohen's messages that later made the rounds of all sections of Israel's Secret Service can be dated from this time – March to July 1963. One Saturday afternoon Elie Cohen heard on the Arabic Radio Service of the Voice of Israel that the Israeli football team had lost an international match at Tel Aviv. He took this defeat as a personal affront, and when he sent off some details on the Syrian Baath leaders to Tel Aviv that evening, he could not contain his patriotic feelings, and added a postscript: "It is time we learned to win on the football field, too. Pass on to the losing team my strong sense of national disgrace."

Meanwhile a new Minister of Information and Culture, Sami el-Jundi,* had been appointed in Damascus. He was a young Baath leader – a tall, thin, energetic intellectual, whose mane of fair hair distinguished him from most Syrians. As a close friend of George Seif, Colonel Salim Hatoum and now of Colonel Salah Dalli (all of whom used his flat for their amours) Cohen had for some weeks past had the free run of the Ministry. Quite often he would sit near Seif in his office while the latter was going through secret reports or receiving instructions from his superiors.

There was, however, one occasion when a minor incident might have produced serious consequences, and this episode discouraged Cohen from carelessly looking over the documents strewn about his friend's desk. A departmental Under-Secretary came into Seif's office unannounced while Seif himself was on the telephone and Cohen was absorbed in a document over-stamped with two diagonal red lines. The Under-Secretary rebuked Seif for letting an outsider read such a confidential document.

Seif was not in the least abashed. He just said: "Don't worry: he's a friend one can absolutely trust." But Seif took the hint and advised his friend to space out his visits to the Ministry and exercise more discretion. The incident was closed, but it had made Cohen go all hot and cold, as he later remarked at Tel Aviv. However, the relations between the two men remained cordial.

Seif's stock was rising since young Sami el-Jundi had become his chief. His job required him to attend most of the public meetings of the Baath party and the civil and military ceremonies organised by the Government. Cohen was naturally only too happy to join him on his various engagements in Damascus or elsewhere whenever he was asked, and in this way

* Later Syrian Ambassador in Paris. He was recalled to Damascus in July 1968 and placed under arrest.

he more than once found himself in a front seat on some important military or political occasion.

Seif himself sometimes broadcast political commentaries over Damascus Radio. These talks might be addressed to the public in Syria or to listeners in neighbouring Arab countries, or again, on short wave, to Syrians abroad, particularly in South America. Cohen was often sitting in the studio next to Seif, whose voice was being heard over the air in Tel Aviv, among other places. The idea was that Cohen-Taabes was taking lessons from his friend in journalism.

During one of these visits to the Damascus studios, Seif made the startling suggestion that Cohen should produce a regular five-minute programme for Syrian emigrants in South America, called "A Former Syrian *Émigré* Speaks". This would be broadcast both in Arabic and in Spanish, both of which Cohen-Taabes spoke perfectly.

The idea for this radio programme had originated in the secretariat of el-Jundi, whose ministerial duties included that of preaching the Baath doctrine abroad. The party was desperately short of funds for propaganda, and hoped to collect money from rich Syrians in Argentina. The ground for this had to be prepared by a press and radio campaign: hence Seif's proposal that Cohen-Taabes, as a former resident in Argentina, should produce and broadcast the programme.

The spy said that he was willing to have a go. Seif then put the scheme up to his Minister, who agreed in principle that Taabes should be offered the job, and asked to see the applicant. The interview was arranged without delay and was exceedingly friendly. Cohen-Taabes made a point of telling the Minister that he proposed to revisit Argentina himself very shortly to raise some capital, adding that he was prepared on this occasion to drum up a collection for Baath funds among his friends.

The following week Sami el-Jundi formally gave his approval to the project, but the spy was in no hurry to accept the tempting offer. He wanted to talk it over first with his superiors in Tel Aviv. So he explained to Seif that it would be better to wait till he got back from Argentina, when he would have deepened his knowledge and renewed his contact with Syrians who lived in Buenos Aires, and would therefore be better qualified to produce the broadcasts.

Shortly before he left, supposedly for Argentina, he had a further occasion to let Tel Aviv know of a major change in the leadership of the Syrian Army. He had found out from one of his friends that the Chief of the General Staff, Ziyad el-Hariri, had been surreptitiously thrown out, and was now under house arrest somewhere in Damascus. It was the Government's intention that, having been deposed, this officer should go into exile. (He left on "sick leave" on July 8, 1963.)

In due course it became known in Western countries that Ziyad el-Hariri was in fact exiled to Paris, but well before this time the news had reached Tel Aviv via Elie Cohen. He was one of the few men in Syria who not only knew that the Chief of Staff had been removed but just why this action had been taken. El-Hariri had talked too much about his ambition to take over the leadership of the Government, and officers opposed to him had passed on a warning. The Government accordingly forestalled him, by sacking him from his job and paying his passage to France, where he passed his exile in relative comfort.

Since 1963 the young General, with a resplendent moustache and laughing blue eyes, has been living in Paris on a Government allowance, with the use of a green Peugeot 404 car with a diplomatic number-plate belonging to the Syrian Embassy. He was for quite a time a notable figure among the "everlasting students" attending Professor Vernant's courses at the *École Pratique des Hautes Études* having turned down the offer of a Syrian Embassy in South America.

A year after Ziyad el-Hariri had been pushed out, Elie

163

Cohen had occasion to mention his name again. Syria had just decided to train special terrorist commandos for use on Israeli soil. General el-Hariri, in Paris, was instructed to get busy recruiting Arab students in Europe, especially students born in Palestine. Damascus proposed (as Elie Cohen recorded in one of his 1964 messages) to incorporate a certain number of Palestinians living in Europe in the terrorist units later known as "el-Fatah".

One final political development was to be observed by Cohen before he left for Israel in the summer of 1963: General Amin el-Hafez, the former Military Attaché in Buenos Aires, who had rapidly moved up the ladder of Baath party leadership, emerged at this point (July 27) as the country's "strong man", and was made "President of the National Council of the Revolutionary Command". This high-sounding title, equivalent to Head of State, was not enough for him. At the same time he appointed himself Military Governor, Commander-in-Chief of the Army, and President of the Baath. Later he even became President of the Regional (i.e. Inter-Arab) Baath Leadership. (The party has an important branch in Iraq.)

Cohen sent el-Hafez a huge box of chocolates, and wrote on the accompanying visiting card "Delighted that your dreams have come true at last." This gesture was promptly rewarded: the spy received an official invitation to a large reception at the Mohajerin Palace, where the General had established his residence. Among the Syrian officers in full dress uniforms and the formally-attired foreign diplomats, the Spy from Israel was to be seen clinking glasses with his friend George Seif and the latter's Minister, el-Jundi.

He did nothing to draw attention to himself, but he could not stop a press photographer from immortalising President el-Hafez's smile as he shook hands with "his repentant emigrant". Cohen boldly asked the photographer to send him a print, and suggested that a group of el-Jundi, George Seif and himself together would be equally worthy of record. The spy had been struck by the idea of presenting the photographs he had ordered to the Dervish when they met some weeks later in Tel Aviv.

The frequent changes in the Army and party leadership had the effect of cutting him off from one important source of information. Maazi Zahreddin had to resign his commission soon after his uncle, Karim Zahreddin, lost his position as Chief of Staff. He complained bitterly to Kamal Taabes; later he was given a lowly job in the Ministry of Local Government.

The evening before he left for Israel, Cohen arranged another lively party in his flat. His suitcases were already locked, ready for the journey, and his friends gave free rein to their high spirits and their pleasures. They had all turned up, including Colonels Hatoum and Dalli, who begged Kamal Taabes to do them another favour by leaving them the key of his flat while he was abroad.

He had to explain that George Seif also used the flat when he was away, and suggested that they should arrange between them to take it in turn. He knew of course that none of them would have the slightest interest in the two well-concealed transmitters in his flat. All they wanted was his bed.

Two new female stars made their first appearance at an orgy in Kamal Taabes's flat that night. One was a young Italian air-hostess employed by the Syrian airline. She had a pretty face but was a bit on the plump side. The other, Colonel Hatoum's latest girl-friend, was none other than the popular singer Loudi Shamania, known to every Syrian who watched television.

To secure her favours, Hatoum had exerted all his influence to get her on Syria's television screens with the maximum frequency. This had not endeared him to his brother-officers nor to President el-Hafez. There had been repeated protests from religious quarters in Damascus against the im-

M

moral behaviour of the singer, whose ambition was unbounded. However, Hatoum, for the moment, was too strong for them. Loudi Shamania, whose voice was far from attractive, thus became the undisputed star of Damascus Radio and television, and the wags of the capital nicknamed their national broadcasting station Hatoumgrad.

At 6 a.m. next day Cohen left his flat. Colonels Hatoum and Dalli were still in his bedroom with their mistresses. He resisted a strong temptation to take a picture of the two couples asleep in his bed. He did not want to risk being caught by one of the Colonels and stupidly wrecking a valuable relationship that he had built up for a special purpose. Anyhow, his assignment was in no way concerned with photographs of this kind, that could have been used for blackmail in other circumstances.

He had an airline ticket for Buenos Aires, which took him initially to Paris. Three days later he arrived in Israel.

18

POINTS FOR DISCUSSION IN ISRAEL

The agent in Damascus asked the Israeli Secret Service one question that summer: whether he should accept or reject George Seif's offer to produce a regular programme on Damascus Radio for Syrian emigrants in South America. The decision rested with "Head Office" and, in particular, with the Dervish.

Tel Aviv weighed up the pros and cons. By accepting the proposal and thus becoming an official employee of the Syrian Government, the spy would greatly strengthen his public status, and thus widen his contacts among Baath supporters in Damascus still further. But the broadcasts would not only be heard overseas; they would also go out over medium wave to listeners in Syria. By drawing attention to himself he would increase the risk of detection.

Someone might recognise his voice. Or the Syrian Security Service might make serious inquiries about his past, which would certainly end in the collapse of the bogus identity that he had laboured to build up. Once he surrendered his position of relative obscurity for the popularity his broadcasts might bring, the possibilities of failure – utter and complete – were inevitably enhanced.

The Dervish had yet another reason for rejecting George

Seif's offer. In his broadcasts to South America the spy was bound to appear as an official propagandist for the Baath. But what would happen when an Opposition *coup d'état* forced the Baath out of power? All in all, the Dervish's view was that Seif's proposal should be turned down.

However, Elie himself disagreed. "Syria", he said, "is in such a state of confusion that no one will have the time or the energy to bother about me. I believe it's quite safe to accept. What's more, I suggest that we make use of these broadcasts. All we have to do is to fix on a key-sentence which would convey to you, for instance, that a state of alert has just been proclaimed in Syria."

The men higher up in the Secret Service were impressed by his confidence and, after prolonged discussion, it was resolved that the spy should be allowed to produce the proposed radio programme. His suggestion for making use of these broadcasts, as well as of his own secret radio, in emergency was likewise noted, but to Elie's regret, the Dervish scored a partial victory. Head Office agreed that Cohen should broadcast on Damascus Radio, but urged that his contribution should be reduced to a strict minimum. He could take part in broadcasts to South America, but must avoid becoming an accredited producer of a regular service.

Cohen had to accept the compromise. He did not like it, but he was under orders, like a soldier. The Dervish then got working on a series of Arabic phrases which Cohen was to use, for the ostensible benefit of his future listeners in South America, but in some instances the phrase would convey a meaning known only to him and Head Office.

Elie drafted a detailed report on his work, just as he had on his previous home leave, and again had the help of his messages from Damascus, recorded and dated. As usual, his capacity for recalling the minutest details of past events astonished his colleagues.

His offer to follow up the information he had gleaned from Rademacher with further inquiries into ex-Nazis in Arab States was again flatly rebuffed by Tel Aviv. He was told bluntly that he was not in Damascus to hunt Nazis. His military and political assignments were infinitely more pressing.

His abilities presented Head Office with a problem. On the one hand he was regarded as the best secret agent that Israel had in Syria, supplying first-class political, economic and military Intelligence over the widest field; so the people in Tel Aviv were under strong temptation to ply their man in Damascus with more and more questions and to set him increasingly dangerous tasks. On the other hand, it was plainly essential to make sparing demands on an agent of such value, and not to expose him to dangers which risked bringing his assignment to a sudden end.

The Dervish kept on telling him that he, Elie, must keep them on the right track. "You're the only man," he said, "who can draw a line between what is feasible and what isn't, between the possible and the impossible. You must tell us, whenever you feel it necessary, that you can't answer this or that question, or that it's impossible or too risky to carry out an assignment we're giving you."

Elie Cohen listened to the sound advice thus formulated by the Dervish and other senior colleagues in Tel Aviv. But he retained an unshaken belief that he was perfectly safe in Damascus and had absolutely nothing to worry about.

Elie's second child was born shortly before he got back to Israel – another girl, whom they called Irit. He would have preferred a son. Indeed most Israeli fathers prefer, or at least say they prefer, their wives to bear sons; possibly a man-child is regarded as a symbol of his father's manliness or maybe he is considered as a contribution to the country's defence, for if

Israel is to survive it certainly needs male citizens. Even so, Cohen was happy to hold his second little girl in his arms, and liked to spend as many hours as he could at home in Bat-Yam "with my three women" – as he used to put it to his friends.

Nadia had been somewhat distressed in the last weeks, not knowing whether her husband would be back in time. She clearly suspected at this stage that he was somewhere in Europe busy with something concerned with Israel's security. But she could not guess that in fact he was so close to home – very near, but in fact completely isolated.

Another problem Cohen's "Head Office" had to deal with was that he had told his Syrian friends that he was off to Argentina. He must really go there, after his leave in Israel, so the practical arrangements were made. In case he failed to raise enough money in South America for the support of the Baath cause (as he had promised to do before leaving Damascus) funds on which he could draw up to a specified limit were made available to him in Argentina.

Once more the time came for him to leave Tel Aviv, to stop off in Paris, to see Salinger and to fly on to Buenos Aires. One of his first calls there was on Alheshan, the editor-in-chief of the local Arab weekly, whose son Kamal had written from Damascus about his friend's intended trip and plans. Not only Alheshan, but other Syrians in Buenos Aires had been expecting him; so Cohen wasted no time. He arranged two private gatherings, which brought together several dozen local Syrians who supported the Baath, and collected from them a total of 9,000 dollars – not a large sum, but enough to convince his friends in Damascus of his good faith.

He promptly announced that he would contribute one thousand dollars to make up a round figure. So within a matter of days Cohen could produce a cheque for 10,000 dollars drawn on an account opened in the name of the Baath at a reputable Buenos Aires bank. He promised the contributors that he would hand over the cheque to General el-Hafez personally.

The spy then spent a further thousand dollars that Head Office had earmarked for the purchase of a mink coat for the General's wife. As a wealthy businessman devoted to the Baath party and its present leader, whom he knew personally, Elie could afford the expensive luxury of bringing back such a generous gift for Madame el-Hafez from a trip in which business was combined with propaganda.

In Buenos Aires he was careful to call on a number of businessmen of Syrian origin whom he urged to import Syrian products into South America. He promised them that the Ministry of Foreign Trade in Damascus would give them practical assistance, asking them to be sure to mention his name. "This," he assured them, "will make it easier for you to deal with officials in Syria."

He felt that letters of this kind would afford additional evidence that during this trip abroad he had, in fact, been promoting Syria's interests. This was really more than an excuse: it was, in a way, perfectly true.

Now he was getting ready to leave Buenos Aires for Damascus with two definite questions to answer:

First, Tel Aviv had some grounds for thinking that Syria was about to receive fresh Soviet war material, including Mig 21 fighters, faster and more powerful than the Mig 19s previously threatening Israel. Light naval craft armed with Komar missiles, such as the Egyptians already had, were also thought to be included.

Secondly, the Syrian scheme for diverting the waters of the Jordan seemed to be passing from the theoretical to the practical stage. There was a danger of Israel's major irrigation plans being wiped out. The spy was urgently required to find out all about this sinister scheme from his friends at the top of the Baath organisation.

So Elie Cohen took off by air via Munich on his return journey to Syria at the end of that summer, with a 10,000-dollar cheque for the Baath party, a mink coat for the wife of its leader – and pressing instructions from the Secret Service of Israel.

19

THE LAST TRIP HOME

Once he was back in Damascus, Kamal Amin Taabes called on President Amin el-Hafez and handed over the 10,000-dollar cheque for the Baath party. The President showed no embarrassment about his wife's acceptance of a mink coat as a present from this supposedly rich Syrian from Argentina; such gifts are common enough in Arab countries. He thanked him for the donation to Baath party funds, and said he would send a formal acknowledgement signed by the party officials.

Taabes got into touch with George Seif at once, and said he would be glad to broadcast to Arabs living in South America, though increased pressure of business made it impossible for him to produce a regular programme. Seif agreed to this loose arrangement, and between October 1963 and the following summer Kamal Amin Taabes gave a number of talks on Damascus Radio to "brother Arabs far away" in South America. His delivery was clear, and the technical staff thought well of his broadcasts, which basically consisted of appeals to Syrians abroad to support propaganda campaigns for the "Revolutionary Baath Party" in their various countries.

These broadcasts – there were no more than a dozen in the whole of 1964 – were picked up in Israel, but he was never

173

instructed to use them for his real work. The invaluable service that he rendered his country during that time depended on the continued use of his secret transmitter. From the autumn of 1963 to the summer of 1964 he was concentrating his efforts almost exclusively on the Syrian scheme for diverting the waters of the Jordan. He was repeatedly ordered to throw everything else aside and answer (as he managed to do) three essential questions – *what* precisely the Syrian scheme was; *when* it would be put into action; and *how* it would be carried out.

Following the decisions of the Arab summit conference held in Cairo under Nasser's chairmanship at the beginning of 1964, the Syrians were going to apply themselves to implementing the plan for water diversion. The problem was to find out the details of their scheme.

Cohen's most reliable sources of information were Colonels Hatoum and Dalli. From these two officers, who had intimate knowledge of Syrian planning, the Israeli spy gathered the main outlines of the scheme. It involved digging a canal right along the high plateau of Syria (known as the Golan Plateau), so as to channel the waters of the River Banias into the River Yarmuk, in Jordanian territory, a tributary of the Jordan with an annual flow of 100 million cubic metres (22,000 million gallons). From the Israeli point of view it was a devilish scheme.

Cohen was not satisfied with just this bare outline. However, the wide range of contacts that he had in Damascus gave him access to two men responsible for putting the plan into force. One was a Lebanese engineer called Michel Saab, who was in charge of the construction of the canal itself. Cohen met him over a hotel dinner with Colonel Hatoum, who had the job of planning the military defence of the canal, and Saab explained its exact topography: it was to extend 44 miles along the Golan Plateau.

Cohen passed on to Tel Aviv, word for word, a phrase

used by Hatoum about the advantages to be gained from Saab's construction work: "What Syria or Jordan do with the water they divert doesn't matter much; the whole point is that it will be lost to the Israelis."

The other man who was particularly useful to him was a Saudi Arabian public works contractor called Muhammed ben Landan, whose acquaintance he made in much the same way. This man, with his fleet of American bulldozers, was in charge of the excavation work. He provided Cohen with details that he had not been able to get from Hatoum or Saab, and added one piece of information which was most valuable to Israeli Intelligence, i.e. that the Syrian Government had commissioned a Yugoslav civil engineering concern called Energo-Prospekt to supervise part of the work.

Cohen gradually pieced the facts together, and over the course of months he was able to build up for his own senior officials a complete picture of the Syrian scheme, including a sketch of the Banias–Yarmuk canal, the timing of the work – it was to take 18 months – and the arrangements to erect a powerful pumping station on the banks of the River Banias that would raise the water up to the canal 800 feet above the level of the river.

All this useful information put the Israelis on the alert. They decided to employ every means available to prevent the scheme from being carried out. Cohen's reports, recorded on tape at Tel Aviv and translated into military terms, were as valuable to the General Staff (which had plenty of opportunities for delaying the Syrian plans, and took full advantage of the fact) as to the Israeli Government.

Another major problem became obvious in 1964, and Israel became increasingly preoccupied with it. This was the formation of Palestinian terrorist commandos, later known as "el-Fatah". Elie Cohen was the first to give Israel the news that the Syrians had resolved to create such an organisation.

This force, controlled by the head of the Syrian Military Intelligence, Ahmed Sweidani (who became Chief of Staff in 1967), brought together snipers, saboteurs and guerillas in fair numbers. Its object was to carry out acts of violence on Israeli territory, and the scheme was closely connected with the water problem, since the primary purpose of the Damascus Government was to destroy Israeli pumping-stations and irrigation canals.

As Cohen found out in the course of 1964, a dozen Palestinian, agencies, controlled by Damascus, were recruiting Palestinian Jordanian and Syrian strong-arm men. Later, the Syrian General Staff used these men, some of whom were given military training in Algeria, as the cadre for two crack commando units which were provided with a permanent base-camp at Kuneitra, roughly 30 miles from the Israeli border. By May Cohen had collected sufficient data on the build-up of the force to report to Tel Aviv. The Israeli Army took immediate action by establishing security controls all the way along the main Israeli irrigation canal and doubling the guard round all hydraulic pumps.

These defensive measure were strikingly successful. There were dozens of attempts to wreck the Israeli irrigation system, but El Fatah saboteurs did not once manage to penetrate Israeli territory in depth, and no damage was ever done on a scale serious enough to stop the southward flow of water from the Sea of Galilee to the Negev desert.

It should be remarked that one day – in March 1964 – Hatoum went to the limits of indiscretion by showing his friend Kamal Amin Taabes a plan of the Israeli canal network, pointing out the exact spots which were "to be blown up one of these nights", as he put it. The Israeli spy immediately sent a report to Tel Aviv, and somehow things didn't work out as arranged.

On three separate occasions between February and October 1964 Elie Cohen was privileged to observe the remarkable scale and strength of the fortifications that the Syrian Army was continually constructing on the plateau overlooking the Sea of Galilee along the frontier with Israel. Each time he was with Maazi Zahreddin, who still had the status of a reserve officer. They made a tour of the high ground and inspected the massive construction work that was to turn this plateau into another Maginot Line.

On each occasion he saw Soviet technicians directing the work; they figured among the countless teams of experts that Moscow had been sending to Syria since June 1963. One site he visited was the command post of the Southern District at El Hama, where he spent a night in the officers' lines. On another sortie he had the opportunity of visiting the Command Headquarters of the whole area, at Kuneitra, where he acquired knowledge of military and strategic data of the highest importance to the Israeli Army Command.

Here are a few headings from the Intelligence file that contained Tel Aviv's reports from its agent in Damascus between February and October 1964:—

Detailed description of concrete casemates designed as concealed emplacements for Soviet-made guns with a range exceeding 15 miles;

Detailed description (with accompanying sketch-plan by Cohen) of fortified trenches several yards deep, designed to conceal the movement of armoured vehicles and tanks;

First-hand reports on the progress made in delivering 200 Soviet T 54 tanks, mainly intended for the Israeli front;

Syrian military planning in the event of hostilities with

Israel – basically a thrust by tanks and armour across Upper Galilee, to cut off this part of Israel from the rest of the country;

Finally, a series of photographs (the first to be docketed by Israeli Intelligence) of Soviet Mig 21 fighters delivered to Syria in 1964.

The assistance that the Israeli spy received from the unsuspecting Colonels Dalli and Hatoum and Lieutenant Maazi Zahreddin was certainly decisive. But there were other officers and civil servants in the Ministry of Defence, and friends of Taabes among the leaders of the Baath, who contributed a good deal to the contents of these files – some of which found their way to Tel Aviv carefully hidden in the drawers of Syrian tables exported to Munich.

Still, it is better not to mention the names of those in Damascus who unintentionally gave the spy their help. Some of them are still members of the group in power in Syria. However it should not be forgotten that Ahmed Sweidani, then head of Syria's Military Intelligence and subsequently Chief of the General Staff*, was one of the sources of the "Israeli Sorge".†

In November 1964 Elie Cohen paid his last visit to Israel. Again, this coincided with a joyful event in the life of the lonely spy – the arrival of his third child. This time Nadia bore the son they had wanted so long. The baby was given the name of Shaul (Saul), and Elie Cohen, wild with joy, wanted to invite all his Secret Service colleagues to the circumcision ceremony when the child was a week old. He had to be convinced that this was out of the question: a gathering of that kind would inevitably have led everyone in the little town of Bat Yam to reflect on how the unassuming traveller for an import–export firm was really employed when he was "somewhere abroad".

* He ceased to be Chief of Staff in the Spring of 1968, attempted a coup in August that year, and fled to Baghdad when it failed.

† Richard Sorge, the spy who won the confidence of the German Embassy in Tokyo during the Second World War and passed vital information to Moscow.

Elie treated himself to three weeks' home leave. After completing his usual detailed report and hours of discussion with the Dervish, he took his wife away for a long week-end in the luxury hotel built by Baron Edmond de Rothschild at Caesarea. Neither the tourists staying there, nor the Israeli golfers who used the local course, nor the owner of the charming seaside restaurant (the Straton) can have guessed the identity of this handsome man, with such intelligent yet gentle eyes, who walked for hours allong the shore arm in arm with his wife.

There was, however, one man who had an inkling, then, about what Elie Cohen really did. This was his brother Ephraim, who told people after Elie's death how he got the idea. "Elie," he said, "had brought us all presents, as he always did when he came back to Israel. This time he gave me a fine pair of shoes. When I put these on for the first time, I noticed that the size was marked with an Arabic character in red ink that someone had tried to rub out.

"I pointed this out to Elie, who had told us that he'd come from Europe, and asked him how it was that shoes sold in Europe had their size marked in Arabic characters. He was obviously put out, and said that he'd made a stop in Turkey and got the shoes there. I didn't say anything, but I knew that this wasn't true. They haven't used Arabic script in Turkey for years."

Nadia and the rest of his family had noticed that on this visit Elie was nervous, depressed and weary; he seemed in no hurry to go off abroad again. One night at Caesarea he admitted to his wife that he was tired of being separated from her and the children. "I've got one more trip abroad, but next time I get home I won't go away again." There was no next time.

"Head Office" had a tricky problem to settle for Cohen. Sheikh-el-Ard, who had become deeply attached to young

Kamal Amin at their first meeting, and had maintained an unbroken friendship with him for three years, had firmly decided to marry him off.

"It's a sin to stay single," he told Taabes. "You're quite wealthy; you've got a pleasant home and a good position; and you've turned yourself into a real Syrian. Time you got married!"

Nor did he stop at that. One day in the summer of 1964 he introduced Taabes to his friend Abu Mahmud, a most reputable fellow-landowner, whose 19-year-old daughter Yasmin asked for nothing better than a husband like Kamal Amin.

Cohen had to humour them up to a point. He met Yasmin and her father several times, and once took them to Beirut for the week-end. But it wasn't a game to be played indefinitely; a decision had to be taken. Neither the girl's father nor the Sheikh would tolerate a prolonged flirtation.

He explained the situation to his superiors and asked for their advice, mentioning something that happened just before he left Damascus. Abu Mahmud, some of whose land had been confiscated by the Government, had offered him 10,000 dollars if he could get his friends in the Ministry of Land Reform to give the property back. Taabes had refused the offer and delivered a patriotic sermon imbued with his idealism "as a loyal member of the Baath party of the Arab Revolution". This only increased the unhappy father's esteem for his son-in-law to-be.

Elie's seniors gave serious attention to his predicament: it was not the first time that they had been faced with a problem of conscience such as this. Ought the spy to be committed to marrying a Syrian girl with whom he was not in love, but who might serve to strengthen his position in an enemy country? Must the private happiness of a spy be sacrificed once again to his country's cause? Elie Cohen had just become a father for the third time: he loved his wife and family . . . In the end they dodged deciding. The Dervish told him to let things drag on:

The special military court. The president Colonel Salah Dalli is third from the left, and on his left is Colonel Hatoum.

Martyrs' Square, 19th May, 1965.

"Avoid answering definitely. Don't say no. Don't say yes."

Elie also accepted another suggestion made by the Dervish. This was that he should buy a car in Damascus to make his work easier. Elie made excuses: he didn't need a car; everyone in Damascus walked. However, he promised to buy a second-hand Volkswagen for not more than 700 dollars, and took this sum with him from Israel.

But he never bought the car. He never had the time. In the last days of January Nadia had a postcard from him to say that he was making a stop in Brussels. Early in 1965 she received a New Year's card from him posted in Italy. These were the last two direct messages that Nadia had from Elie, apart from his final letter, written before he died.

20

CAUGHT

It was eight o'clock on Thursday morning, January 21, 1965. Elie Cohen had just tapped out a message to Tel Aviv. At dinner the previous evening with Colonel Salim Hatoum, he had found out that President el-Hafez had called a meeting of senior officers of the Syrian Intelligence Service to discuss a plan for merging the various Palestinian organisations. According to Hatoum, el-Hafez favoured the formation of a single "Palestinian Commando Brigade" under Syrian command for sabotage operations in Israel. With the war in Algeria as a model, the President suggested transforming their own struggle with Israel into what could be represented as a Palestinian "People's War" to win back "their own" territory.

Having sent off his despatch, the spy, sitting on his bed, had switched on his radio receiver, and was waiting for the instructions from Tel Aviv that were usually sent him as soon as his own message had been recorded. His miniature transmitter, which he had taken out of its hiding-place (as he did every night and morning), was still beside him on the bed. He should now have heard a characteristic crackle from the radio set, showing that Tel Aviv was on the air and about to send him their message.

At that very moment there was a loud bang on the outer door of the flat. Before he could take any action, the door was smashed in. He was now on his feet, instinctively shielding his tiny transmitter with his hand. Eight plain-clothes' men burst into the room, pointed their revolvers at him and ordered him to put his hands up. Dozens of Syrian Security men – though he did not know this – had cordoned off the block.

A strongly-built officer in army uniform whom Elie already knew, was in command – Colonel Ahmed Sweidani, head of the Syrian Intelligence and Counter-espionage Services. The Colonel thrust his way through the group.

"Caught in the act, you damned spy." He made no effort to conceal his anger and his joy.

"*Dakhilkum!* (Please!)," said Cohen calmly. "What's the trouble? I am an Arab from Argentina."

The Colonel rapped out: "Save your breath. What's your real name?"

"Kamal Amin Taabes, a returned emigrant from Argentina," Cohen persisted.

"Very well," growled Sweidani. "You needn't bother. You'll talk in good time."

Later on, the Lebanese weekly *Al Asboua Al Arabi* published an interview with the Colonel in which he said:

"I am still amazed at the naïvety of certain of my countrymen in letting themselves be fooled by Elie Cohen's stories. They really believed that he was going to send their goods to Europe, and were convinced that he had opened a Damascus branch of an export–import firm that was going to become one of the most prosperous businesses in Syria. They all imagined that Cohen had unlimited bank accounts in Switzerland and Belgium at his disposal, and were delighted to accept his expensive presents in return for the excellent information they fed him with.

"I, personally, took charge of the investigation and interrogated Elie Cohen myself. My suspicions about him were aroused as soon as I was given – unfortunately at a very late stage – a list of the people who regularly visited his flat. Most of them were men in high positons in the economic, political and military life of Syria. I was particularly struck by the case of one individual (whose name I must not reveal), who was known to have very wide contacts in influential circles in Damascus." (Is he perhaps alluding to Hatoum? Or to Maazi Zahreddin? He does not give any further clue.)

"Our inquiries regarding Cohen were not confined to this particular individual. We shadowed and investigated everyone who was in the habit of visiting the flat. At first we ran into a good many difficulties, largely because Cohen had gone about his work with such remarkable discretion.

"For instance, he didn't keep a maid; he cleaned his flat himself, did his own laundry and even polished his own windows. We also discovered that he never met the same people in the daytime that he met at night. For certain visitors he had an agreed signal, and didn't open his front door unless the bell had been rung a given number of times.

"After we'd pressed our inquiries far enough to take action, we kept the block under observation and traced the aerial on his roof. We timed our forcible entry to his flat at eight in the morning so as to catch him in bed. The idea was to make sure he couldn't defend himself or try to commit suicide by jumping out of his fourth-floor window. Three of our men were to occupy his room, while a fourth kept a tight hold on him in bed. The whole operation was not supposed to take more than two or three minutes.

"However, Elie Cohen had a surprise in store for us. When my men burst open the door, he was already awake and waiting for a radio message from Tel Aviv; his transmitter was on the bed beside him. What is more, we found a slip of paper on which he had made notes for the text he had just sent, with the words 'Will send further report.' Cohen kept assuring us that he was an Arab emigrant back from Argentina."

This personal account by Colonel Sweidani of Cohen's arrest is plainly a concocted narrative. The man at the head of the Military Intelligence always has his own reasons for not letting out the whole truth in such circumstances. Contrary to Sweidani's statement, Cohen had not aroused the suspicions of the Syrian Security Service in the least: neither he nor any of his friends had been shadowed by agents.

The truth is simpler and less romantic. Two or three days before the Israeli spy was arrested Sweidani had been provided with irrefutable proof that an illicit transmitter was operating in the district where Cohen was living. It was only after bearings taken in this area pointed to a transmitter located in that particular block that Sweidani and his men were convinced the transmitter could only belong to Cohen. When they surrounded the block that Thursday morning and broke into his flat, they certainly intended to catch a spy actually on the job.

While the Colonel and his senior assistants kept Cohen stading in the bedroom, well away from the searchers, others turned the flat upside down and put their hands on the second transmitter. Knowing that Hatoum and Dalli were among Cohen's closest friends, Sweidani must have realised what a steady stream of Intelligence reports, all stemming from the best sources, had flowed through these transmitters from Damascus to Tel Aviv.

Raging with fury, he spat in Cohen's face, cursed him, and demanded to know who the other Zionist spies in Damascus were, and where the other transmitters were hidden.

Cohen pale but composed, replied "Two transmitters were all I needed."

The Security staff unearthed explosive powder hidden in a cake of Yardley soap and three tiny packets of deadly cyanide.

Sweidani commented, "I suppose you thought you'd have time to commit suicide before you were arrested. But we shall decide when you're going to die."

Meanwhile the most recent films that Cohen had taken and was about to forward to Israel were being laid out on the sideboard, and with them several cheque-books and the whole of his correspondence with Salinger.

Cohen answered one question about the explosive: "I had no intention of using it for any sort of sabotage in Damascus. If you hadn't been too quick for me, I'd simply have blown up my transmitters. That's all."

Sweidani was in no doubt that he'd caught the spy in action, but he firmly believed that the man was an Arab using an assumed name and working for the Israeli Secret Service. That he was dealing with a genuine citizen of Israel simply did not occur to him.

Unluckily for Cohen, the Colonel had an inspiration: the spy must get busy and send his "Head Office" a new batch of messages, but they were to contain information dictated by the head of Syria's Military Intelligence.

During the next three days and two nights Sweidani and half a dozen of his men never left the flat. The Colonel and his deputy, Second Lieutenant Adnan Tebara, conducted the interrogation, while the others kept watch. At this stage Elie Cohen was not tortured in any way.

At eight o'clock that Thursday evening Sweidani, with his revolver trained on Cohen, drafted a message of no great consequence, which the spy had to cipher and send off to Tel Aviv; the gist of it was that the Syrian Army was in a state of alert. Cohen called up Tel Aviv, and after the usual brief pause the acknowledgement came. Tel Aviv was standing by to receive Damascus.

One can well imagine the intense eagerness of the spy, at this moment of drama, to warn Tel Aviv that he had fallen into enemy hands. The morse signals he sent over the air were his last link with his country and the men for whom he worked. It was only a matter of time now before the link was broken – and there was a revolver at his back.

He tapped out the message at his normal speed, making no effort to hoodwink the Syrians. Uncertain whether they knew the cipher he was using, he did not introduce any variations. But imperceptibly, with unruffled self-control, he succeeded in slipping into the middle of the message a signal, too subtle to notice, which he could be sure would be understood in Tel Aviv: it was just a very slight variation in touch, a sort of change in rhythm that would be detected at the other end. In this way, even in this message sent under duress, he still managed to convey the truth. That alteration in touch meant – and this had been the signal agreed before he left Israel – that Elie Cohen had fallen into enemy hands.

The Secret Service Headquarters at Tel Aviv was plunged in gloom that night. The operators assigned to pick up Cohen's messages put their finger on the agreed signal at once, and passed on the alarm to the men at the top, including the Dervish. It was unmistakable: there it was, as it were in black and white, on the tape that they played back more than once over a loud-speaker. The touch was different; it said clearly: "They've caught me."

However, one message tapped out under the muzzle of a revolver was not enough for Sweidani. Next day, the Friday, Cohen was compelled to send off another. This time the spy did not risk giving the prearranged signal. It would have served no purpose. When acknowledgement came from Tel Aviv, Cohen must have realised that his superiors had understood from the signal the previous night that their best agent was in Syrian hands. As picked up by Cohen and deciphered by his captors, it read: "Reception bad last night and this morning; try to repeat your messages tonight."

Evidently, Tel Aviv was quite aware of what had occurred in Damascus, and was joining in the game Sweidani was playing. Sweidani, however, was convinced that the Israelis had not got a clue, and had fallen into the trap. So on the Friday night Cohen was ordered to repeat the two earlier messages which had suffered "bad reception". This time he took advantage of Sweidani's critical over-confidence, and again changed his touch, so as to convey his warning undetected: "Disregard anything I send; I've been caught."

Sunday came – January 24, 1965. By President el-Hefez's personal orders Damascus Radio broadcast a formal announcement of the capture of the spy Kamal Amin Taabes. Shortly before the news went out, Tel Aviv got its last message from their agent, dictated as before by Colonel Ahmed Sweidani and transmitted by Cohen. Here is the text:

"For Prime Minister Levi Eshkol and Secret Service Chief, Tel Aviv, from Syrian Counter-Espionage Service. Kamal and his friends now our guests in Damascus. Assume you will send us all his colleagues. Will give you news of his fate shortly."

That was the last sound that was heard from Elie Cohen's miniature transmitter in Damascus. The message was deciphered in Tel Aviv and passed on at once to the Prime Minister, who received it less than an hour before Damascus Radio broadcast its news of the capture of the Spy from Israel.

The men in power in Damascus reacted to Cohen's arrest in a very different manner from the jaunty tone of Sweidani's message to Eshkol. The news, still secret, that Kamal Amin Taabes had been caught, reached el-Hafez and Colonels Hatoum and Dalli in the course of the Thursday, and completely bowled them over. They tried, for one wild moment, to persuade themselves that Seidani had cooked up some fantasy of his own, but they had to bow before the evidence: Taabes had admitted that he had been working for Israel.

Once this was established, they resolved to protect themselves. They had had sustained and (so far as the Colonels were concerned) very close contacts with Taabes, an agent of Israel, and now that he had stumbled, they might well fall. As soldiers they knew that attack was the best defence. So President el-Hafez decided to make a public announcement that this master-spy had been caught, before rumours of his arrest got round Damascus.

On the President's orders Hatoum and Dalli joined in the interrogation that Sweidani's assistant, Adnan Tebara, had been conducting in Cohen's flat since Thursday morning. From their point of view this was the best way to wipe out the recollection of how and in what circumstances they had made the spy's acquaintance there.

At dusk on January 24 Cohen was moved under escort from his flat to the 70th Armoured Brigade base outside Damascus. He was locked up in a narrow cell without artificial light, the type normally used for military offenders. Around ten o'clock that night he was marched into the Commandant's office, where he found President el-Hafez seated with Sweidani. Standing there, in front of the President, whom he had known in Buenos Aires and met on various occasions in Damascus, the spy is believed to have disclosed his identity, though it was not made public till the following day: "Elie Cohen from Tel Aviv, a soldier in the army of Israel."

Some weeks later, el-Hafez himself gave an account of this dramatic confrontation to a special correspondent of the Beirut weekly All Asboua Al Arabi:

"Not long after Elie Cohen's arrest by the Syrian Security Service I saw him in prison. The first impression was that we were dealing with a genuine Arab called Kamal Amin Taabes who had been recruited in Argentina by the Israeli espionage organisation with a view to sending him to Syria. But when I looked into his eyes, I had doubts about his being an Arab. I put several questions to him relating to the religion of Islam, which seemed to puzzle him, and I asked him to recite the Fatha (the first chapter of the Koran, which is also used as a Moslem prayer), and he could not get beyond the first few lines. He excused himself by saying that he had been very young when he left Syria and no longer remembered the prayers.

"I then realised that my doubts were well-founded, and that he was a Jew, not an Arab. When I asked him other questions about religion, he did not answer. This was not the first time that I had questioned a Jewish spy in the course of my military duties, and I had some experience of this type of interrogation.

"After seeing Cohen in prison, I issued orders to the Intelligence officers in charge of him to direct their inquiries into the new field I had opened. Next day they came and reported that Kamal Amin Taabes was really an Israeli spy called Elie Cohen. I had several later meeings with Cohen, who refused the cigarettes I offered him, and did not drink. He showed complete self-control and behaved with courage and dignity in these distressing circumstances."

El-Hafez knew just what those "distressing circumstances" were. Once Cohen had been transferred to 70th Brigade base camp, he underwent four weeks of torture. He was repeatedly subjected to the diabolic torment of having electric contacts applied to the most sensitive points of his sexual organs and nostrils. His nails were pulled out, one after another. (The treatment inflicted on his hands and nostrils was apparent in the television coverage of the trial.) But as el-Hafez observed in his interview, Cohen retained his dignity and courage. With all their torture, the Syrians did not succeed in breaking his spirit.

The authorities in Damascus were indefatigable in their efforts to turn the spy's capture to their credit. What they hoped for was to convince the other Arab States of their own watchfulness; what they could not obscure was the fact that an agent had been allowed to operate in Syria for three years – and the degree of his success was notorious.

Meanwhile, they pressed on with the arrest of batches of Syrian citizens who had had some kind of connection, close or remote, with the spy. Dozens of people who had had nothing whatever to do with him, but were known to be hostile to the régime, were rounded up at the same time. During the week that followed Cohen's arrest, more than 500 people, all living in Damascus, were thrown into gaol. They included 17 women, among them members of the Radio and Television staff, a Syrian air-hostess, several secretaries from Government offices and a few society ladies.

Sheikh Majd el-Ard, Maazi Zahreddin, George Seif and other personal friends of Cohen who did not enjoy the privileged immunity of Hatoum and Dalli were naturally arrested. The two Colonels had been quick to put them under lock and key so as to prevent stories of the celebrated nocturnal orgies in Cohen's flat going the rounds in Damascus.

However, from February 1965 onwards, the wildest rumours circulated. Wagging tongues spread ridiculous tales about the incredible Spy from Israel who had managed to insinuate himself into the highest circles of the Baath movement. in these stories the adventures of the "Jewish fiend" generated both horror and admiration.

Damascus newspapers fed the flames by expatiating on the tremendous triumph of the Counter-espionage Service in revealing "the most important Israeli spy ever unmasked in an Arab country". The Beirut newspapers improved on this, and one large daily, *El Hayat*, headed a report of its inquiries: "DAMASCUS' MORNING DECISIONS RADIOED BY COHEN EACH NIGHT."

The torturing of Cohen in his military prison outside Damascus continued meanwhile, and he was questioned for hours about his life, his past and his superiors in Tel Aviv. The interrogators were never certain whether he had been working alone in Damascus or with accomplices. But they discovered something that no newspaper in Damascus or Beirut ventured to print, namely, that Cohen had not been caught as a result of any brilliance and efficiency on the part of Sweidani's Counter-espionage Service, but by pure chance.

How, in fact, had he been caught? Israeli and other experts who have studied the case are unanimously of the opinion that one can rule out any idea of betrayal. He had no accomplices in Damascus. He had, as we have seen, made use of quite a number of Syrian citizens, especially men high up in the Government and staff officers. Gradually and quite unintentionally, they came to co-operate with him. But not one of these men had suspected Cohen of spying for Israel; still less could they have guessed that he himself was an Israeli citizen.

Any possibility of Cohen having given his deadly secret away to someone or other can equally be ruled out. He was naturally reserved, loyal to his organisation, devoted to his country. He had allowed only one person in the world to gather what kind of activities he was engaged in: his wife, Nadia. Even she did not know precisely what he did or where. So the conclusion must be drawn that Cohen was caught by mere chance, though the chance was combined with a technical development perfectly designed to facilitate detection within a special field.

To clarify matters: when Cohen used his transmitter twice a day, he caused some slight radio interference in the immediate neighbourhood of his flat, which was in a building facing the Syrian Staff Headquarters. A number of foreign embassies and consulates (including the Indian Embassy) had offices in this district, and all of them used transmitters and receiving sets.

There were therefore days when radio reception and transmission at the Indian Embassy suffered interference from Cohen's use of his transmitter. This was drawn to the attention of the Syrians, who proceeded to conduct a survey of the whole neighbourhood without finding anything unusual and without any special concentration on the block where he lived.

However, the interference persisted. This seemed odd, and experts at Staff Headquarters considered that it pointed clearly to "someone" in the area using an illicit transmitter. The Counter-espionage Service consulted the Soviet experts who had been in Damascus for the past two years, and on their advice the Syrian Army acquired for its Intelligence staff an up-to-date Soviet van for locating radio direction. This vehicle contained electronic apparatus with antennae that could determine the bearings of any transmitters operating within a radius of several hundred yards.

This van started patrolling Damascus early in January. Whether Soviet technicians or Syrians were operating it is not known, but it is a reasonable guess that Soviet experts were keeping the operation under close supervision.

The vehicle functioned most effectively when it patrolled the streets of Damascus during periods of electricity "black-out", preferably total. This is the point at which Elie Cohen blundered; being no doubt beguiled by excessive confidence, he took no notice of an incident which – as we can recognise with hindsight – was the prelude to his capture.

Two days before his arrest he had informed Tel Aviv that on the preceding night he had found difficulty, not in sending a message from his battery-run transmitter, but in picking up Tel Aviv's message on his receiving set which was run off the main. This was because, as he said, "there was an electricity breakdown over the whole of my district".

Cohen, who was always so well-informed and always had the answer ready to any question his seniors put to him, had not worried about this electricity failure. But it was not an ordinary failure. The Counter-espionage Service, investigating his neighbourhood, had arranged for an electricity cut while the tracking vehicle made a tour round the embassies and Staff Headquarters. We know now something that Elie never learned: on the night of the electricity cut that he had reported the Counter-espionage people had turned an entire block of flats in his vicinity upside down, in the belief that one of the tenants there was operating an illicit transmitter.

Nothing more happened for two days. Did Sweidani and his staff have a hunch about Taabes, or did something point in his direction? There is nothing to prove either theory. However, on the Thursday morning a fresh "black-out" afflicted the Abu Rumana district. This time Cohen was unaware of it: at eight in the morning he did not have the light on in his bedroom, and the battery-fed set he used for transmitting to Tel Aviv was independent of the mains supply. He had no time, when he switched on his receiving set, to observe that it was not working for lack of current. It was just at this point that Sweidani and his Counter-espionage personnel, having at last tracked down the illicit radio that was interfering with local transmitters, burst into his flat.

21

THE BEST OF THEM ALL

The broadcast from Damascus Radio, monitored in Beirut, was duly telegraphed to the *New York Times*, where a couple of paragraphs were printed on January 25. These stated simply that Syrian Intelligence quarters claimed to have discovered "a dangerous espionage ring" working for Israel; the leader and members of the ring had been arrested and had confessed, but the broadcast had not given their names or nationality. One point was made, however: initial investigations showed that the ring's activity was connected with "the tough Syrian policy towards Israel" and the activity along the Syrian-Israeli border.

Equally brief reports appeared in Tel Aviv newspapers. Anyone in the know was naturally inclined to play the arrest down. Since Syrian broadcasts were apt to claim the capture of an Israeli spy roughly once a month, most people disregarded the announcement.

However, on January 26 something more specific appeared in the *New York Times*. Their Beirut correspondent had telegraphed the previous day as follows:—

"A Jew posing as a Syrian emigrant from Argentina was reported today to be head of an Israeli espionage ring un-

195

covered in Syria. He was identified in *Al Baath*, the newspaper of Syria's ruling party, as Elie Cohen, who was said to be masquerading under the Arab name of Kamal Amin Taabes."

As soon as this report had been published, the Prime Minister of Israel, Mr. Levi Eshkol, called a meeting in Tel Aviv of the managers and editors of all local dailies, and informed them of the Government's intentions. They hoped, he said, with the help of friendly countries and prominent men abroad, to be able to save Cohen's life.

"Civilised States," said Mr. Eshkol, "no longer execute spies. The normal procedure is to arrange an exchange of agents or, at the worst, to inflict a term of imprisonment. We shall do everything in our power to save Cohen."

He asked newspapers not to publish anything further, thus allowing the authorities to proceed discreetly with all the measures required to save their agent. After they had questioned the Prime Minister on Cohen and his activities, the Tel Aviv newspaper managers promised to refrain until further notice from publishing anything likely to impede the steps that were being taken.

A major political and diplomatic campaign was then launched on a world-wide scale to save Cohen's life. Every Israeli embassy abroad was alerted. Diplomats, special representatives of the Israeli Foreign and Defence Ministries, private individuals – all set to work on influential friends in the various countries to arouse public opinion and thus bring pressure on the Government of Syria. Two months later the trial of Cohen came to an end, and it subsequently became known that, despite every effort to avert it, the death-sentence had been passed. The campaign was renewed with redoubled energy – but in vain.

It is worth recalling just a few of the international names enlisted at some point in the campaign from January onwards (right up to May 18, the date of Cohen's execution). All of them

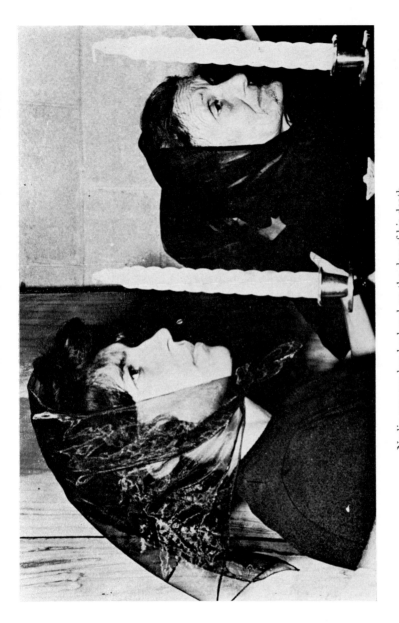

Nadia mourns her husband on the day of his death.

David Ben-Gurion personally attends the mourning ritual (*shiva*) with Nadia Cohen and her family.

drafted or signed petitions or issued public appeals, and some of them made direct approaches to the authorities in Damascus:—

Pope Paul VI; Giorgio La Pira (then Mayor of Florence); Antoine Pinay and Edgar Faure (both former French Prime Ministers); the late Queen Elisabeth of the Belgians; the late Camille Huysmans (a former Belgian Premier, who offered to go to Damascus and plead with President el-Hafez for clemency); John Diefenbaker, the former Prime Minister of Canda; the International Red Cross; and an incredible number of parliamentarians, senators, journalists and leading men in every field from the United States, Scandinavia and South America.

Cardinal Felcius of Buenos Aires wrote from hospital to President el-Hafez: knowing that he himself was on his deathbed, he asked that his letter should be regarded as a kind of last will and testament. However, el-Hafez was not moved by appeals from the dying Cardinal or anyone else. It should be remarked that even a Communist Member of the Israeli Parliament, Dr. Moshe Sneh, the party leader, responded to the appeal of the Government of Israel by making a tour of the East European countries with the result that approaches were made to Damascus from several Communist capitals. But their pleas, too, fell on deaf ears. Damascus had no wish to listen; long before the trial it had been decided that the Spy from Israel, who knew too much about the régime and its leaders, must die.

The police investigation lasted a month: Cohen was brutally tortured from late January till the end of February. Only on the last day of that month was it announced by Damascus radio that the trial of Elie Cohen before a "Special Military Court" had just begun. The composition, prerogatives and powers of this court had been laid down in a decree of the Presidential Council dated January 7, 1965. One of its five members was Colonel Salim Hatoum, and the presiding judge was Colonel Dalli.

No Counsel was allowed to attend the Court's sittings;

except in the opening stages, no journalist was allowed into the hearings, which took place in a building adjoining General Staff Headquarters. Excerpts from the proceedings were given over the Syrian radio and television in due course, but this applied only during the first few days to parts of the examination of Elie Cohen, Sheikh Al-Ard and Maazi Zahreddin, who were all on trial together. Nadia Cohen and the Government of Israel had briefed two French barristers to defend Elie – Paul Arrighi, the *bâtonnier* (Chairman of the French Bar Council), and Jacques Mercier – but neither was allowed in court.

Thus, the case was tried *in camera*. But evidence subsequently made available and extracts from the transcript of the proceedings, most of which was published in the Lebanese press, make it plain that it was a travesty of judicial procedure.

At the opening session Choen stated again that he was "Elie Cohen, a soldier in the Army of Israel." He then asked to be defended by Counsel. Colonel Dalli, the President of the Court, snarled back: "You don't need a lawyer. You're being defended by all the corrupt newspapers in certain Arab countries. Your most ardent protectors are the enemies of Syria's revolution."

Cohen was asked the names of his accomplices, and said that he had never had any. When he was pressed for the names of his friends and acquaintances in Damascus, he reeled off a long list. But he did not at any point mention the names of his judges, Hatoum and Dalli, though they had been among his closest friends.

The hearings went on from Ferbruary 28 to March 19, with one week's recess. At one sitting Colonel Dalli told him to point out Colonel Hatoum. Cohen turned round and looked towards the far end of the court-room where a group of officers were watching the proceedings. Then he turned back to Dalli and said: "Colonel Hatoum is not here."

This was one of the incidents in the trial that were

televised; many people in Israel, including Nadia, saw it on their sets.* Obviously, this particular episode was not shown to the public by chance. There is good reason to believe that at some stage in the examination and questioning of Cohen by Dalli and Hatoum an understanding had been reached whereby the spy was promised his life, provided he kept quiet about the names of his two cronies, now his judges. If this was so, only Dalli and Hatoum reaped some temporary benefit. Their hour was to strike, but much later.

Another day Cohen was asked with what government departments in Damascus he had been in regular contact. His answer was "The Ministries of Defence and Information, Damascus Radio, the Central Bank and the Ministry of Local Government."

He had been alone in the dock when the case opened, but within a few days he had 36 other accused persons sharing it with him. They had been selected from the 500 people arrested after his capture. Besides Maazi Zahreddin, Sheikh Majd el-Ard and George Seif, those charged included nine women, of whom one was a Syrian air-hostess alleged to have illegally conveyed messages from Cohen to his superiors in Europe and Israel.

Maazi Zahreddin was asked by Dalli: "Why did you never suspect this man of being a spy? He was always throwing money around, but didn't do any work." To this Maazi replied: "I suppose I'm not very bright."

George Seif was asked: "Is it a fact that you used to have the key to this spy's flat, so that you could send messages to Tel Aviv from time to time in his place?"

Seif's reply was: "That's not true. I borrowed the key to meet girls in his flat, and I wasn't the only one." Dalli, who knew better than anyone who had used that key and why, made no comment on Seif's indirect charge.

Cohen more than once renewed his request for a defence

* Israel itself had at this time no television service.

Counsel, and was invariably rebuffed. At one point Dalli exploded to his fellow-judges: "What? Are we expected to provide a lawyer for this spy who managed to give the Israelis the exact locations of our guns and tanks all the way along the frontier? Who else could have been responsible for the Israelis' being able to train their fire right on our positions?"

Colonel Dalli knew what he was talking about. In November 1964, at the time of Cohen's last visit to Israel, there had been a violent clash on the border with Syria. Served by first-class Intelligence, the Israelis had managed to wipe out by shelling and mortar-fire not merely a number of Syrian military positions, but also the tractors and bulldozers digging the canal that was intended to divert the waters of the Jordan. It was Cohen who had produced the extremely accurate plans of the engineering work.

During all the weeks between his capture on January 21 and his execution on May 18, Cohen was allowed only one civilian visitor – a Lebanese journalist, who published in *Al Asboua Al Arabi*, at the end of May, a statement that he was supposed to have made:

"I want it to be known that I have not betrayed Israel, and that in Syria I devoted myself to working on behalf of my country's Intelligence Service, in the hope of making the future of my fellow-citizens, my wife and my three children secure."

Damascus Radio and Television had given Nadia Cohen more than one glimpse of her husband during the trial, and she had heard Elie's voice in the dock reproduced. On March 5 she left for Paris to take a personal part in the strenuous campaign to save his life. She applied to the Syrian Ambassador to France, George Seif's former Chief, Dr. Sami el-Jundi, but he refused to receive her. A French lawyer brought him her written request on March 6, but his answer was: "I knew Elie

Cohen and now realise how dangerous he was. I can do nothing for him."

France-Soir published a short interview with Nadia the next day, but neither her plea "to save my husband, the father of my children" nor the efforts of hundreds of men of good will all over the world had the least effect.

Five young Arabs, spying for Syria, were arrested in Haifa by the Israeli Counter-espionage Service on March 7. Their names were at once published and the Israelis offered to release them together with other Syrian agents, arrested earlier and serving prison sentences: they would free the lot in exchange for Elie Cohen but this proposal was not even answered. Damascus was plainly not interested in the fate of the Syrian spies. They had only one desire – to obliterate the very memory of Elie Cohen as soon as they could.

The trial ended on March 19, but the verdict was not delivered till May 1, and it was only a week later that the sentence was published in Damascus over the signature of Colonel Salah Dalli as President of the Special Military Court. Here is the crucial passage:

"Whereas the accused, Eliahu Cohen, Son of Shaul Cohen, alias Kamal Amin Taabes, penetrated into the El Al Zone, which is deemed to be a closed military zone, and whereas he penetrated into this zone with intent to collect secret information to be communicated to the enemy, of a kind prejudicial to the security of Syria, we sentence him to death by hanging."

Maazi Zahreddin was condemned to five years' hard labour, Sheikh el-Ard to ten years' hard labour, and George Seif to five years' imprisonment without hard labour.

More than a month had elapsed between the conclusion of the trial and the announcement of the sentence. It looks as if the Syrian leaders hesitated to take a decision that even in their eyes must have seemed something of a crime. President el-

Hafez felt stronger doubts than any of the others; he may have been moved by a letter from Paris in which Dr. Kuss, the surgeon who had operated on him in the American Hospital at Neuilly at the end of 1964 and saved his life, pleaded with him "in the name of life to spare the life of Elie Cohen".

But el-Hafez was reluctant to show mercy. In the situation that prevailed in Damascus his own position was already highly uncertain. He may have been afraid of being attacked for his moderation, if he gave way to temptation and spared the life of the Spy from Israel. Be that as it may, el-Hafez, who was no doubt under pressure from the fanatical Sweidani (who had been another of Cohen's informants), never responded to any of the appeals for leniency. It was el-Hafez who finally confirmed the sentence and sent Elie Cohen to the gallows.

The sentence pronounced on May 1 and made public a week later came as a severe shock to the two French barristers, Arrighi and Mercier, who had taken it in turns for the past three months to pay visits to Damascus in the frustrated hope of being allowed to see Cohen. A report distributed by the French news agency at the end of March recorded that they had notified the International Commission of Jurists, then in session at Geneva, that the rights of the defence were being denied, since the Special Military Court allowed no barrister or attorney to be present.

"Maître Arrighi and Maître Mercier (the communiqué went on), who earlier telegraphed their views to the President of the Syrian Republic, are asking for a fresh trial in accordance with procedure that guarantees the rights of the defence. The French defence Counsel have never been allowed to see Cohen or to attend the sittings of the Court, but they have been given the assurance that the Syrian President will receive them before he takes any decision . . ."

When this despatch was published on March 31 the trial of Cohen had ended twelve days before, and the verdict had been decided for practical purposes, though it was (as we have seen) not pronounced formally till May 1 or made public for a further week. Cohen's lawyers, excluded from the trial, only gradually discovered these facts through the newspapers and radio.

On the Saturday night (May 8), just before the news of the death sentence reached Europe or Israel, a high-minded Frenchman who had made his own attempt at saving the Israeli spy got back to Paris, worn out from his efforts in Damascus. This Frenchman, a retired Colonel, who had spent years in Damascus and was married to a Syrian woman, knew President el-Hafez personally and suggested going to Damascus to "ransom" Cohen. Some quick work at Geneva and a night journey from there to Paris provided him with a cheque on a Swiss bank for *a quarter of a million dollars*. He was authorised to promise Syria, in addition to this sum, tractors, bulldozers, medical equipment and ambulances. But the Colonel did not manage to get his audience with el-Hafez. The President was afraid to meet him. Rather than say "No" to the offer, he had preferred to turn an old friend away from the door.

Half an hour after the Colonel had got back to Paris, the news of the death sentence came over the radio. The Israeli Ambassador, Walter Eytan, heard it while visiting friends in Montparnasse. He rushed back to the embassy in the Avenue de Wagram, hoping even at this stage to get the decision reversed. However, it is not easy at ten o'clock on a Saturday night to get hold of Ministers or public figures or even one's friends in Paris. Still, next day Mr. Eytan managed to get in touch with Pierre Mendes-France and Edgar Faure, both former Prime Ministers of France. Finally he got hold of Georges Pompidou, the Premier himself.

A flood of telegrams from all over the world poured into Damascus, but Damascus paid no attention. Once more Maître Arrighi and Maître Mercier were fobbed off with promises which by now no one believed. Meanwhile Elie Cohen, waiting in his cell, did not even know what his friends, his countrymen, his family and countless foreigners were trying to do to save him.

May 17, his last day, came. At ten that evening the ghastly announcement from Damascus radio was picked up by other stations: "Elie Cohen is to be hanged in the course of the night." The First Secretary of the Israeli Embassy in Paris, Joseph Hadass, was attending an important meeting of barristers and various legal and political advisers. He leapt to the telephone and passed on the bad news.

Then he turned to Arrighi, the Head of the Paris Bar: "You must save him. The Syrians have let you down."

The barrister had not quite lost all hope. "But what can I do now?" His voice was distraught.

"Phone the Vatican." Arrighi did so, and a cardinal promised to do the impossible. Meanwhile Maître Mercier tried to get through to the President's Palace at Damascus. The call came through only at eight next morning. Too late, just as General de Gaulle, whom M. Pompidou prompted that night, intervened only when it was all over.

For it was during that night of May 17-18, 1965, that Elie Cohen was roused in his cell by Colonel Dalli, that he recited the prayer for the dying with the Rabbi of Damascus, that he wrote his last letter to his wife, Nadia, and in the small hours was hanged in the main square.

The two French barristers, Mercier and Arrighi, addressed an open letter to President el-Hafez on May 24, summarising the shifts and false promises with which every attempt to secure either a fair trial or a pardon for Elie Cohen had been blocked (see Appendix). Maître Mercier commented more bluntly at the time to an Israeli journalist in Paris. "He was done to death like a dog," he said, "brutally murdered by men without pity."

The Syrian Government had not even acceded – as the two barristers had hoped they would "out of mere respect for human dignity" – to Nadia's request that her husband's remains should be delivered to her care. Why this final piece of cruelty? They can hardly have been afraid that this extraordinary Spy from Israel, for whom they had hurriedly found a grave in the Jewish cemetery of Damascus within hours of his execution, would rise from the dead.

The International Red Cross asked for the return of his body to Israel. Syria refused – and still refuses. In July 1967 Israel handed back to Syria all the prisoners taken in the "Six Day War", and asked in return for Elie Cohen's remains. Another refusal. When a peaceful settlement is reached one day between Israel and Syria, one of its conditions is likely to be that Elie Cohen's body shall be returned from Damascus to his country.

Nadia heard of her husband's execution over the radio. Blind with rage, she smashed the set, gnashed her teeth and broke every window in the house. Overcome by her helplessness, she burst into tears and finally lost consciousness. For the next three days and nights she was never more than half alive.

Colleagues of Elie met at his home, and the Head of the Israeli Secret Service addressed them:

"In our calling there always comes a point at which we ask ourselves what our limitations are as individuals. Elie refused to ask himself such a question. He was a pure idealist, always aiming a little higher, always going further than the next man. We knew him to be the best man of all of us, the best man one could possibly imagine.

"I seem to hear among us voices calling for vengeance upon the Syrians for their barbarous cruelty to Elie. But I think we shall be best avenged by the success of others – many others – who will follow where Elie Cohen has led."

The Head of the Secret Service was justified in his prediction: others did follow where Elie Cohen had led. The whole world realised this when Israeli forces reached the high plateau of Syria in 1967 and captured El-Hama and Kuneitra, which Elie had known well. Israeli tanks got within 30 miles of Damascus: Elie Cohen and those who followed where he led had played a major part in giving the Israeli Army complete knowledge of the ground.

And what of those who inflicted death upon Elie Cohen? President el-Hafez, overthrown by Baath extremists on February 23, 1966, is still in prison somewhere in Syria. Colonel Dalli, Elie's former friend who became his merciless judge, was brought before another special military court on March 29, 1966, and charged with high treason. He, too, is languishing in a military prison somewhere in Syria. Colonel Sweidani, as related earlier, was involved in an abortive coup in the summer of 1968 and is now in exile in Baghdad.

As for Colonel Hatoum, his fate was the grimmest of all the men responsible for the death of the Spy from Israel. He had taken part in the *coup d'état* of March 8–9, 1963, and that of February 23, 1966 (which brought down el-Hafez). He was one of the men who plotted a fresh coup on September 8, 1966, which miscarried. Hatoum took refuge in Jordan, and when war broke out with Israel in June 1967, he seized his chance to get back to Damascus, But this time he did not escape: he was immediately arrested, sentenced to death on June 25 and shot next day.

APPENDIX —

Text of the letter sent from Paris to General el-Hafez, President of the Syrian Arab Republic, by *Bâtonnier* Paul Arrighi and *Avocat* Jacques Mercier, the French barristers who had undertaken Elie Cohen's defence, but were not allowed to see him or attend the trial.

"Monsieur le Président,
Elie Cohen was executed two days ago without our being allowed to plead for a reprieve.
He was convicted and sentenced without our being allowed to defend him.
We have no knowledge of the brief.
We have never seen the accused.
We do not even know whether he died knowing that his family and his countrymen were trying to help him.
Yet we were assured that we should see him, that we should defend him and, finally, that we should be able to ask for his pardon.
Not a single one of these promises was kept.
This exceptional situation prompts us to write to you

for the last time and, with the authorisation of our colleagues at the Bar, we are publishing this letter, so that our final protest shall not pass unobserved.

In January 1965 we were entrusted with the defence of Elie Cohen, who had been arrested in Syria on charges of spying. Maître Mercier then proceeded to Damascus in order to confer with the authorities on how the defence of the accused should be organised. He was received on February 1 by his Excellency Walid Taleb, Minister of the President's Office, who was accompanied and assisted by Mr. Mamoun Atassi, Secretary-General. The following statement was made to Maître Mercier on behalf of your Government:

As Police inquiries had not been completed, it was not possible, by law or precedent, to communicate with the accused. On the other hand, as soon as the brief on the case had been passed to the Public Prosecutor and the Military Examining Magistrate*, the accused's Counsel would be allowed to visit him and take over his defence in accordance with normal practice.

At Maître Mercier's request, it was established that, subject to the decision of the Chairman of the Damascus Bar Council, we should, if we so desired, have access to the Bar.

As soon as Police inquiries were completed, the Secretariat of the Presidency of the Republic would notify us by telegram.

Finally, the Minister undertook to send on to the accused a letter informing him that Bâtonnier Arrighi and Maître Jacques Mercier had been briefed to defend him.

As soon as Maître Mercier returned to Paris we took cognizance of these promises in a letter dated February 4. However, in view of persistent suggestions in the press that the trial was about to open, he returned to Damascus on February 25. On Saturday, February 27, he was received by the Sec-

* Roughly equivalent to Judge Advocate in the British Army.

*retary-General of the Presidency and informed that no change
had occurred since the assurances had been given.*

*It was with utter amazement that he found out by
chance late on the following day (Sunday, February 28)
that the trial of Elie Cohen had already started,* in camera
*and before a Special Military Court set up under an Order
dated January 7, 1965; and furthermore that when the
"hearings" (from which excerpts were shown on Syrian
television) had opened, the President of the Court, Sallah
Dalli, had informed the accused, when he asked for the
services of Counsel, that he was refused any such assistance.*

*It thus appeared that, in spite of the promises given us,
Elie Cohen was unaware that we had been briefed for his
defence; otherwise he would have mentioned the fact.
Moreover, not only were we not notified when the Police
inquiries ended, but further – when Maître Mercier was
actually in Damascus for this very purpose, with the full
knowledge of the Syrian authorities – he was not allowed to
see the accused before the trial, without any legal represen-
tation, began.*

*Our colleague then asked to see his Excellency Walid
Taleb, Minister of the President's Office, who (again accompanied and assisted by the Secretary-General, Mr. Mamoun
Atassi) received him on Monday, March 1. Maître Mercier
lodged a formal protest, on this occasion, against the deliberate
failure to fulfil the promises he had been given.*

*Meanwhile, in answer to a request that had been
forwarded to your Excellency on the previous evening, seeking
at least an interview with the accused, Mr. Walid Taleb
informed our colleague that this would be granted and that he
would be allowed to see Elie Cohen that very day. The Minister
added that consideration was also being given to Maître
Mercier attending some of the hearings as an observer, with
Mr. Mamoun Atassi assisting him as an interpreter.*

In view of the peculiar character of a form of trial that deliberately ignored the rights of the defence, our colleague reserved his decision on this last point until he had spoken to the accused. But on returning to his hotel, where he expected to learn the time and place where he was to have his promised interview with Elie Cohen, Maître Mercier had a telephone call at 1.30 from the Secretary-General of the President's Office to say that the Military Court had unanimously decided that no one was to be permitted to see Cohen. This decision was final. It could not be modified. Any further discussion was a waste of time.

Maître Mercier, on his return to Paris, informed me of these facts, the accuracy of which cannot be disputed. We wrote to his Excellency Walid Taleb, Minister of the President's Office. and conveyed "to the Government of the Syrian Arab Republic our most solemn protest, once more, against administrative and judicial procedures that defy law and morality".

We then asked our colleague Jean Talandier to proceed to Damascus in his turn. He was received on March 20 by his Excellency Walid Taleb, and drew his attention to the fact that even under the terms of Article 7 of the decree of January 7, 1965, the verdict must be submitted to Your Excellency as Supreme Magistrate of the Syrian Arab Republic. The decree conferred on you the power to uphold the sentence or to review the Court's procedure and even its decision. He therefore urged that Elie Cohen's Defence Counsel should be received by your Excellency before any decision was taken.

Maître Tallandier was given the most complete assurance on this point, and told that the trial would probably last another week. But this latter statement was immediately belied by a communiqué announcing that the last televised scenes from the Court had been shown on the previous night (March 19). He got in touch again with Mr. Mamoun Atassi, the Secretary-General of the President's Office, who asserted that the communiqué meant to convey to the general public "that the televised programme was over", which did not necessarily imply that Court proceedings had finished.

Mr. Mamoun Atassi renewed his assurance that your Excellency would take no decision before granting us an audience. That was the situation when we telegraphed you on March 23 in the following terms:

"MAITRE TALANDIER OUR REPRESENTATIVE INFORMS US THAT DESPITE ASSURANCES GIVEN HIM TRIAL SUDDENLY ENDED VERDICT SEEMINGLY IMMINENT STOP WE REMIND YOU ARTICLE SEVEN DECREE OF SEVENTH JANUARY 1965 EMPOWERS SUPREME MAGISTRATE SYRIAN ARAB REPUBLIC REVIEW COURT'S PROCEDURE AND DECISIONS STOP IN NAME OF PRINCIPLES GUARANTEED BY RIGHTS MAN AND SYRIAN CONSTITUTION WE APPEAL TO YOUR EXCELLENCY TO RESUME TRIAL WITH ASSISTANCE COUNSEL AND RECOGNISED UNIVERSAL GUARANTEES"

To this telegram, as to a variety of other letters and telegrams which we addressed previously or subsequently to your Excellency or to other authorities of the Syrian Arab Republic, we have never received an answer.

Maître Mercier then agreed to go to Damascus again, which he did three times more. On the last of these occasions Mr. Mamoun Atassi, Secretary-General of the President's Office, received Maître Mercier on May 11 and confirmed to him on the telephone on May 14 that we should at least be given the chance to plead for Elie Cohen's pardon: a meeting for this purpose on Saturday, May 22, or Sunday, May 23 was being considered. Maître Mercier told me of this last promise when he got back to Paris.

In a final telegram on Monday, May 17, we re-called this promise. In spite of all the promises previously broken, we still wished to give credence to the undertaking we were given. No death-sentence is ever carried out in any civilised country until the defence lawyers have been allowed to submit a last appeal to the man empowered to grant a pardon.

The same evening news reached us from Damascus that Elie Cohen was to be executed that very night.

In view of these facts, we asked the President of the Bar Council of Paris for permission to make an exceptional departure from the rule of silence that respect for justice imposes on members of our profession. To be silent on the travesty of justice in Damascus would be tantamount to sanctioning the most extreme injustice and tolerating contempt for the pledged word and the most sacred rights.

We are therefore making public in this letter our most solemn protest to you against the violation of the promises given us, and against a procedure and a penalty persistently carried out in defiance of every rule of morality.

We must finally add that no single man in any civilised country in the world, whatever the crimes of which he is accused – without even his lawyers being allowed to know what they are – has ever, we are certain, approached the awful moment of his execution in such utter isolation.

Though our protests and request have never aroused the slightest response from the Government in Damascus, we still hope that out of mere respect for human dignity you will accede to the request of Mrs. Nadia Cohen that, together with the last message of the man executed, she shall be allowed his mortal remains.

We have the honour to be, Monsieur le President
    Paul Arrighi, President of the Bar Council.
    Jacques Mercier, Barrister-at-law."